T

AMBASSADOR'S JOURNEY

A PARABLE ABOUT
NONPROFIT BOARD LEADERSHIP

BRIAN BRANDT AND
ASHLEY KUTACH, PH.D.

Authors of BLIND SPOTS:
WHAT YOU DON'T KNOW CAN HURT YOU

Too many of us attend board meetings but we do not really join the board by sharing trust, competence, enthusiasm and commitment. Here is a guide for boards and directors alike to both challenge and encourage the work of each.

Fred Smith
Founder of The Gathering, Fourth Partner Foundation, and Leadership Network

One of the best primers and guidebooks on nonprofit board service I've seen. Brandt and Kutach offer high-level vision, tools for reflection, and practical tips on how to contribute more effectively on boards. A must read and a fun read!

Tom Lin
President and CEO, InterVarsity Christian Fellowship

Brian and Ashley have helped so many leaders through their exceptional training sessions. Now, through this book they are providing a written roadmap for nonprofit organizations to thrive!

Smittee Root
Executive Director, Leadership Tyler

Much more than just a manual of how-to exercises, Brian and Ashley have crafted an entertaining and relatable fictional story that will resonate with board members in various positions. Whether you are new to serving on a board, a veteran volunteer, a board chair or nonprofit staff, using *The Ambassador's Journey* as a team book study will help to create stronger, more effective board members and transform your board's current climate.

Maya Bethany
Executive Director, 1 in 3 Foundation

Having served as an executive director of a nonprofit, chaired nonprofit boards at the national level, and taught nonprofit board governance in masters programs, I can confidently say that *The Ambassador's Journey* is a welcome gift for nonprofit leaders, board members, and students alike. Crafted within an engaging narrative detailing a novice board member's journey from success to significance, Brandt and Kutach have given us a treasure trove of best practices of nonprofit boardsmanship—from onboarding, to conducting effective meetings to, of course, serving as enthusiastic ambassadors for the organizations we serve. A great read and a great resource!

Jay Ferguson, Ph.D.
Head of School, Grace Community School; Board Chair, Council on Educational Standards and Accountability; Board Chair, Association of Christian Schools International; Adjunct Professor, School of Law and Governance, Gordon College and Baylor University

The Ambassador's Journey is a relatable story of why many people love serving on nonprofit boards and why some should never be chosen to serve. The authors have skillfully packed the book with a compelling storyline, mixed with discussion questions to include in your next board retreat or new member onboarding orientation.

Kimberly B. Lewis, MS, CE
President and CEO, Goodwill Industries of East Texas, Inc.

I have had the pleasure of working regularly with Brian Brandt for years on board development and strategic planning with my organization's board. *The Ambassador's Journey* lays out many of the ways Brian has helped our board understand their critical role to the organization and how they can apply their talents and abilities to achieve even greater results for our organization. This book lays out some key principles and challenges and will become one of the resources we use in our future board meetings and orientations.

John English, M.D.
CEO, Bethesda Health Clinic

The Ambassador's Journey is filled with meaningful information for new and seasoned board members. It can be read quickly or in several short sittings with great questions at the end of each chapter. This would be a great book for a board retreat or could be used in small segments at several different board meetings. I will be using it with our board trainings and highly recommend it for boards that you are involved with. It will also be a great tool for anyone to read on their own if they want to strengthen their own ability to be a good member.

Fonda Latham, LCSW, ACSW
Vice-President, Solihten Institute

This book is a wonderful tool for any and all boards and certainly executive directors, too. The story and questions are very thoughtful and would bring out the best in your board and help board members, new and old, reflect on making the most of their service.

Lisa Lujan
Community Volunteer

Highly effective organizations are products of effective boards—the converse is also true. *The Ambassador's Journey* is a nicely written and well-paced parable that guides the reader through all phases of board member, nonprofit executive, and organizational dynamics. The personal reflections, group discussions, and actions presented will help make your organization stronger by creating a better and broader understanding of the distinct and interrelated what, why, and how of each perspective as board member and nonprofit executive.

Dennis Cullinane
CEO, East Texas Food Bank

Brian Brandt and Ashley Kutach weave board leadership principles into an evolving narrative as they follow one member's migration from tentative engagement to mature influence. Any individual new to board membership should take *The Ambassador's Journey* to arrive at a full understanding of expectations in board involvement.

John Ashmen
President, Citygate Network

Core Insights has created a compelling look into the roles of impactful board members as Ambassadors! As an executive director, I have utilized their first book, *Blind Spots*, as a professional development tool with huge success. I will be utilizing this book to create a robust, engaged board full of Ambassadors!

Stephanie Taylor
Executive Director, Alzheimer's Alliance of Smith County

Brandt and Kutach continue their unwavering journey toward an excellent "you" in all endeavors. They simplify and demystify board service to others—at scale, sustainable, and with purpose.
Dr. Juan Mejia
President, Tyler Junior College

As someone serving in my first board chair position, this book has helped open my eyes to how I can better equip and resource board members to be successful in their roles, truly understand the mission of the organization, and see how they can utilize their God-given gifts and talents to impact the nonprofit.
Carrie-Ann Jasper Yearty, PHR, SHRM-CP
Vice-President of People, Jasper Ventures, Inc.

This book is a great combination of an excellent primer for people just engaging for the first time in nonprofit work and at the same time a great reminder to experienced board members to take off their "blinders of experience" by focusing on what is really important in their work.
A.W. "Whit" Riter
President, Riter Management Group and Riter Family Foundation

A great book for nonprofit professionals and board members. The opportunity for significant self-reflection into board service exists in this read.
John Gaston
President and CEO, United Way of Smith County

THE
AMBASSADOR'S
JOURNEY

With sincere appreciation to the men and women who are engaged as board members, board chairs and executive directors, helping their nonprofits thrive and move forward to change the world.

Table of Contents

About the Authors

BRIAN BRANDT has spent his life supporting the transformation of individuals and organizations. He is the C.E.O. of Core Insights, a Texas-based company providing premier training, strategic guidance, leadership coaching, and keynotes for businesses, nonprofits, and associations. His passion is developing stronger leaders and stronger organizations based on his three decades of leadership experience, including roles such as a C.E.O., public relations director, national sales director, executive pastor, and college tennis coach. Brian has served nonprofits as Executive Director/C.E.O., and now as a consultant providing board training, executive director and board chair coaching, strategic planning facilitation and speaking at special events. He regularly speaks on leadership topics including: blind spots, leadership, effective communication, nonprofit issues, and how to bring a vision to fruition. He is consistently interviewed for radio, television, and print media outlets and has written on a wide range of leadership topics. Brian holds a Master of Global Leadership from Fuller Seminary in California, as well as a Bachelor of Accounting from the University of Oklahoma. Brian volunteers for and serves on the board of numerous nonprofit agencies.

ASHLEY KUTACH, PH.D., has a passion for helping people and serving others, both in her career and in her personal life. An accomplished facilitator, executive coach, consultant, keynote speaker, strategic Human Resources leader, volunteer, mom, wife, and nonprofit board leader, Ashley provides a perfect balance of compassion and grit in her down-to-earth conversations with others. Her powerful stories, pertinent examples, and on-point suggestions not only spark action but touch the hearts of those with whom she interacts. Ashley currently serves as the Vice President of People at Mentoring Minds, an education resource company and is active in nonprofit leadership within her community. Ashley holds both a Bachelor of Arts and a Master of Arts in Communication from Texas State University and a Ph.D. in Human Resource Development from the University of Texas at Tyler. She has spent over 20 years inspiring individuals and businesses to aim high and then take steps to make their goals a reality. She believes that discovering and addressing blind spots is a critical key to success.

Visit www.CoreInsightsLeadership.com for more information.

Introduction

We love seeing nonprofits accomplish their mission because we believe nonprofits provide critical services and strengthen communities. Together, we've both served several sides of the nonprofit world. Brian has been the executive director/CEO of an established nonprofit. We've both been board members and board chairs for several nonprofits. As well, we both lead a lot of board retreats and trainings, and we've spoken at conferences for a large variety of nonprofit associations. We wrote from our experiences in hopes that executive directors and board chairs will see the path to lead others to become Ambassadors for their organization. Likewise, we hope board members see how intentionality in their board service is enjoyable, fulfilling, and leads to accomplishing the mission.

There are three basic steps to follow to get the most from this book:

Read and Enjoy—This book was written as a parable to provide a creative and enjoyable way for board members to grow. As you read the story, we hope you'll see aspects of yourself in the various characters.

Reflect—At the end of each chapter, you will find personal reflection and group discussion questions for board members. As well, we've provided suggestions to put what you're learning into action right away. These suggestions are categorized as

Bronze, Silver and Gold activities, with Gold being the most intense and highest level of activity. Choose the levels that best fit your time constraints.

Also, while board members are the primary target audience for this book, additional reflection questions for each chapter are included in the back of the book that specifically target both board chairs and executive directors.

Learn—You will find even greater value in your reading experience if you engage a learning circle of other board members to work through the book with you. Learning circles provide an opportunity for you to gather others for input, insights, feedback, and accountability. A learning circle may involve meeting regularly with a few select fellow board members online or at a local coffee shop. You can even reserve a few minutes before or after your regular board meetings for discussion. The more you invest working through the discussion questions and challenges presented in the book, the more benefit you will gain.

We encourage you to take time at the end of each chapter to thoughtfully consider each question, meet the challenges presented, and if you are reading the book along with a group, engage in group discussion.

ONE

The Big Announcement

IT WAS 1:34 P.M. on Friday, October 14. Chris Stevens had finally wrapped up the big project he'd sought to complete that week. It was now time to coast through the rest of his Friday afternoon and head home.

He closed the door of his office, opened Spotify, started his favorite Bob Dylan album, and straightened up his desk. A stickler for keeping his life orderly and organized, Chris then looked at his calendar and reviewed his to-do list for the following week. As he gazed out his seventh-floor window, it didn't take long before he started daydreaming about his plans for the weekend.

Jayden, now four years old with a birthday on the way, had soccer practice at 9:00 a.m. the next day. Chris, himself a decent athlete, had been coaching Jayden's team for the last few months ever since the previous coach transferred to Chicago.

"I'm already going to all of the games and practices. I might as well jump in and coach," Chris had offered to the delight of the other parents one day. Chris didn't know much about soccer but supposed he could learn enough to satisfy the skill level of four-year-old children. Secretly, Chris had hoped that as his son grew older he would take up running—Chris's favorite sport and hobby. He dreamed of the day father and son could do a 10K together. But for now, soccer was a fun way to spend time together outside and meet new people.

Chris took a moment to ensure he had printed out the starting team roster and noted which parents had responsibilities for snacks and juice boxes that weekend. Everything was in order. "I might even slip out a little early today," Chris thought, although wrongly, as he checked his email for the tenth time that day.

One new message caught his eye and sent a little shiver down his spine. Jennifer, the vice-president of human resources and strategy, had sent a 4:15 meeting request to all senior leaders, managers, and directors at Sharp Edge Marketing, the mid-size firm where Chris worked. The subject line was labeled, "High Importance." Jennifer had allotted 30 minutes for the update. It was strange for her to schedule a meeting at the last minute, especially on a Friday afternoon.

Chris's gut told him somebody was getting fired at 3:45, and the rest were going to hear about it. Or worse, a massive layoff was coming down the pike.

The rest of the firm was soon buzzing quietly like bees deep in the trunk of a tree. Everyone was hoping a 3:45 meeting invite didn't pop up on their calendars that included them, their immediate supervisor, and Jennifer.

Chris texted Emily, his wife of eight years, to let her know he would be late.

> **Hi Em! Unexpected leadership meeting at 4:15. Not sure what's up?!?! May be home late after I run with Michael. Love!**

Then, he cut and pasted a similar message to Michael.

> **Unexpected leadership meeting at 4:15. Not sure what's up?!?! Still planning on 5:15 run, but I'll text you by 5 if I need to delay. C u soon...I hope!**

Emily took a deep breath when she read the text from Chris. Several of her friends had lost their jobs in meetings that popped up late on a Friday. Her level of angst grew quickly, like Mentos bubbling up in a Coke bottle. This level of anxiety wasn't typical for her easygoing nature, but she was beginning to stress for some reason.

"Oh, please don't let this meeting be bad news," she silently pleaded.

Emily was passionate about her work as an independent nutritionist and food blogger, but she wasn't working enough to support their family. Her mind began to race with wild possibilities of what would happen if Chris was suddenly unemployed.

Without even thinking about it, Emily hugged little Jayden as he played in the living room. When he looked up, she forced a smile and kissed the top of his head. Jayden squirmed away from the unexpected distraction from the Legos he was playing with on the living room floor.

Emily tried to change the direction of the conversation going on in her head. She decided to respond to Chris's message.

Can you talk?

Chris called immediately.

"I really don't know anything else..." he started to say.

"Are your clients happy? Have you all lost any big retainers? What are people saying?"

Her questions met with a big sigh from Chris. Emily quit her interrogation and quickly decided to be the consummate encourager instead. "I'm sorry," she continued. "We'll just catch up when you get home. I'm probably borrowing trouble!"

"There's plenty of that going on here, so you're not alone," Chris responded. "I'll text if I hear anything more. Try not to worry until I know more. Love you!" he added, wondering if he should have even bothered his wife by telling her about the meeting. He understood she was worried. But they'd never been ones to hold back much from each other.

"Okay, I'll just wait to get the story when you get home," Emily replied. She tried to be short, sweet, and to the point. Things were going well for them, and she hoped that wasn't about to change. Like a reflex, she texted her neighbor Stephanie.

**How about getting the kids' bikes ready
and going walking while they ride?**

Three minutes passed when she got a thumbs up, and three minutes later they were out the door. Physical activity was her stress reliever, and if she could do it with a friend, it doubled the impact.

Meanwhile, Chris spent the next couple of hours trying to stay away from the gossip pool. Usually the break room and other gathering spots at Sharp Edge were filled on Fridays with light conversation about weekend plans with the family and what series would be binge-watched. But not today!

"What are you hearing?"

"Did we lose the Murphy account?"

"Are you okay?"

"I feel sick to my stomach!"

Around 3:00 p.m., another email came in from Jennifer. The subject line read, "Relax!" and the message allowed Chris to breathe a little deeper.

> It's come to my attention that my email, and the subsequent meeting, has caused quite an unintended stir. I'm sorry. Nobody is losing their job. The company is doing well, but there is a shift that is going to take place, and it matters to me and the rest of our senior leadership. Again, nobody is losing their job! See you soon!

Chris texted Emily with a calming update. He was relieved, but now the meeting especially piqued his interest. "What could be so important that it requires a 4:15 meeting on Friday?" he wondered.

When 4:10 arrived, he was still unsure of what was coming. Chris took his jacket off the back of his office door, looked at his reflection in the window glass, and straightened his pocket square. He opened the door hesitantly, grabbed a Coke Zero from the break room, and headed for the conference room.

The room was already full of "those" people. Chris described them as his colleagues who must not have enough to do since they always arrived tremendously early to meetings. "If you're not early, you're late!" He'd heard their mantra a hundred times!

Chris settled into a chair near the front of the conference room, still conjuring all the possibilities this meeting could entail.

Preston strolled to the front of the room and started his typical comedy relief routine. He was always good for bringing levity. Nobody could quite figure out what he was doing on this day, but it looked a little bit like a combination of Muhammad Ali shadowboxing and Beyoncé dancing.

"Sit down, you clown!" someone joked.

"What in the world are you doing?" another called.

Whatever it was, it made everyone laugh. Preston fed off the heckling and went even more extreme in his antics. He had a great sense for physical humor, reminiscent of Kramer on the television show *Seinfeld*. Suddenly, the look on Preston's face changed, and he sheepishly shut it down and exited stage left as Jennifer rolled in right at 4:15, coffee in hand.

She walked to the front of the room, turning to her team with a slight look of angst, looking like a judge in her courtroom.

Chris got the same sinking feeling as when he'd read the first email. "This can't be good," he speculated silently.

He thought highly of Jennifer and rarely saw her with such a serious demeanor. While not comedic like Preston, Jennifer usually wore a warm and genuine smile. She had been part of his interview process at Sharp Edge and had often provided him with helpful feedback. Jennifer had even mentored him on two projects during his three years at the company.

"Thanks for the warmup act, Preston," Jennifer said playfully. She looked over and grinned at Preston as he made himself as small as his big frame could be, like a turtle retreating into its shell. Chris's shoulders relaxed a bit.

Capturing everyone's attention, Jennifer began humbly, "I'm sorry for the last-minute meeting late in the day and the alarm I unintentionally created. I'm traveling on business for the next few days and want to share something that's on my heart from our SLT retreat." The SLT was the Senior Leadership Team at Sharp Edge. "I also wanted to do it sooner than later, giving you all plenty of time for consideration."

She took a sip of coffee before continuing with growing enthusiasm. "As you know, I—along with the other members of the SLT—recently escaped for a three-day retreat at High Hill Farm in the beautiful piney woods of East Texas where we clarified and codified our values. One of those values revolves around being engaged in and giving back to the community of Austin and surrounding areas."

The tone changed as Jennifer explained, "We've given this lip service in the past, but have not clarified and communicated what we mean." She continued, slowly and firmly, but with intentionality. "We want all employees to share in the giving back to our community. Moving forward, there is an expectation that all those in supervisory positions will choose at least one nonprofit organization, representing an area that you care about, and start volunteering there consistently. Think of a place where you utilize your talent and expertise. We want this to be a cause that you will get behind and serve in a meaningful and impactful way. We can talk about how you can even leverage the resources of our company to help. Those not in supervisory positions will be encouraged to volunteer in their community as well and will receive 16 hours of paid volunteer time each year. Employees can use this time to work while serving others in some way."

Jennifer was focused, and it showed. The resolve in her voice couldn't be missed. It felt like a locker room speech at halftime when the team is down by a touchdown. She moved to the right side of the room and concluded, "To be honest, we're not exactly sure what this will look like, and we want to give you time over the next few months to find a place that fits you, your talents, and your stage of life."

At that point, Kimberlee, a direct report of Jennifer's, hopped up on cue. "I'll be documenting and keeping track of this initiative," Kimberlee said. "Everyone will be expected to complete an online form by December 15 stating their intentions. So, please start thinking right away about how you want to get involved. Furthermore, please note that this will be a part of each person's annual performance review. We believe that we should all be held accountable for making our community a better place to live."

Jennifer scanned her team, and said, "We've got time for a few questions. Who wants to go first?"

Wanda immediately stood up in the back of the room. "I have one comment and one question," she began. "First of all, while this meeting may have been called suddenly, and it did scare the crap out of me, thanks for not rushing us to make a decision. I may only be speaking for myself, but I'm going to need to take some time to find out what my options are. My question is, what is the expectation regarding the amount of time per month we give to this initiative?"

"Thanks, Wanda," Jennifer said. "There's not a specific number of hours we have in mind. We do want the work that you do to be meaningful. And we will give you time from your normal work schedule. As I said, it does need to fit you and your stage of life. As you start to gain clarity on the organization where you'll serve and the role you'll play, those will be the kinds of discussions we want you to have with your direct supervisor. If you volunteer for two hours in July, let's say, and then don't do anything else the rest of the year, that likely won't be meaningful, right? But we're also not asking you to forsake your family and your work."

Brad raised his hand at that moment and asked, "What if we're already actively volunteering with a local nonprofit? You made it sound like we have to find a new one."

Jennifer made a face as if she'd just seen a snake. "Oh, no. That's not it at all. I know many of you are active in our community. I'd say just make sure that you're leveraging the resources of Sharp Edge. Let's explore ways to collaborate and maximize impact, but please do keep on with what you're doing, Brad!"

Chris raised his hand. "I coach my son's soccer team. Is that the type of volunteering you are suggesting?"

Jennifer paused for a moment before responding. "It is wonderful that you are coaching, and I have no doubt that the work you are doing is meaningful both for you and the players. The answer depends on if your work is impacting under-served and under-privileged people in our community. We want you to look deeply at our community needs and serve that population through a nonprofit organization. If the team you coach is part of a nonprofit initiative, and serves others who meet these criteria, then certainly that work qualifies. If not, there are many other organizations out there to choose from."

"Ugh," Chris thought. He hardly believed the middle- and upper-class kiddos showing up to soccer practice in their parents' new SUVs qualified as under-served or under-privileged. He was disappointed that the hours of volunteering he was already doing weren't going to count toward this new requirement and decided to press a bit further for understanding. "I'm genuinely curious. Why is the requirement limited to a nonprofit organization serving a particular population when there are so many other ways we can contribute to our community?"

Jennifer knew this was a tricky question to answer. Nonprofit organizations serve many critical and important roles in a community. They often target the basic needs of the most vulnerable citizens, but not always.

"Coaching your neighborhood team is important," she explained. "But it likely will not impact the community in the same way as volunteering in a role that serves vulnerable members. We want you to go outside the comfort of your own neighborhoods and reach people who not only need help but are also people you would likely never meet otherwise. You may have the opportunity to mentor, guide, and impact lives in a way you never thought possible. I doubt you're spending any work time on coaching, Chris. We'd hope you'd continue to coach but add something that leverages you to make a profound impact."

Chris understood Jennifer's point, but he wasn't happy about the thought of finding time in his schedule to do something that he sincerely didn't want to do.

The meeting concluded after Jennifer answered a few more specific questions. Chris's thoughts were all over the map. He was certainly relieved that nobody got the hatchet. The mandate for all supervisors to get involved with a nonprofit organization seemed strange for a business, but it did fit the strong, caring culture of Sharp Edge.

To be honest, Chris didn't have a specific passion for any particular nonprofit and wasn't sure this requirement should be forced upon him. Between work, family, and coaching soccer, time was already tight.

He was glad he was going on a run right after work. Chris always gained clarity on issues during a scenic run, especially when his good friend Michael came along to ask great questions and provide insight. Running also allowed Chris some time to unwind a bit before he got home.

The men initially met one day in the parking lot of Zilker Park. Chris had already seen Michael several times on the trail, so he knew they often ran at the same time. Their pace seemed to be similar. Chris decided to introduce himself, and the two had been running partners ever since.

Today's rendezvous point was just outside the doors of Michael's upscale condo on Lady Bird Lake. Michael pointed at his new shoes as he gave Chris a big hug. "Check out these new beauties, and speaking of beauties, I've got dates with two this weekend."

Chris rolled his eyes and shook his head.

Chris and Michael had a great friendship, but they were more different than they were alike. Michael, a successful 48-year-old personal injury attorney, was coming off his third divorce. He hardly ever showed up without sporting some expensive new piece of running gear. While Michael was nearly 15 years Chris's senior, they were equal matches at running.

As Chris and Michael headed out for a six-mile run along the lake, Michael asked with a scowl, "So what was up with a Friday afternoon meeting?"

Chris filled him in on all that Jennifer had shared. They ran along steadily, and Michael listened intently as Chris rambled and vented about the new requirement to volunteer for a nonprofit organization.

When a break in the monologue arose, Michael jumped in with a gut reaction. "Give me a break! Someone's feeling guilty at the top and trying to minimize it by making you volunteer. Oh, brother! Get ready to bang your head on the wall a few hundred times. I've served on two boards that were the biggest waste of time, other than my second wife, that I've ever had!"

Chris took advantage of Michael doing all the talking and pushed the pace. But between Michael being in fantastic shape and Chris getting him fired up, Chris's friend didn't look the least bit fazed.

"These organizations moved at the speed of a snail," Michael continued. "We couldn't make a real decision if we *had* to. I'd show up at these board meetings, and it would just be boring committee reports and an update on financials that I hardly understood. Most board members seemed to be there to network with those who might be beneficial to their business or pad their résumé. I quit one board and couldn't wait for my term to expire on the other one."

Michael finished ranting just as they stopped for their turn at a crosswalk. He frowned at Chris and moved his head to the side, gesturing for Chris to look to the right. Chris turned to realize the object of Michael's annoyance—a toothless homeless lady sitting next to the street light with a cardboard sign asking for help. Chris usually avoided corners with homeless people to lessen uncomfortable encounters, but lately it seemed impossible to avoid them. To Chris and Michael, it seemed as if a tsunami of homeless people had arrived in Austin in the past year.

Just then, the woman turned and looked right at Chris. "Thank you in advance!" she said with a grin, not even looking at Michael.

"Um, sure. Have a good day," Chris replied tentatively, having no idea why she would thank him. She hadn't even held out her hand for money. The light changed, and he and Michael started running across the street.

"Do you know her?" Michael said with a questioning gaze.

"Never seen her in my life."

◆

On his drive home, Chris reflected on the conversation with his friend. Michael offered no encouragement and didn't ask any of his usually helpful questions.

Obviously, he'd had a couple of less-than-stellar experiences working with nonprofit organizations in the Austin area. While the information that Michael shared gave Chris some additional perspective, the run was not the clarifying experience he had hoped for. In fact, Chris was even more concerned and confused as they parted ways at Michael's condo.

That night over a new Thai dish that Emily had prepared, Chris shared some details about the work announcement.

"What do you think that means for you?" Emily asked. "What are you interested in doing in the community?"

"I have no idea. At first, I thought maybe the soccer coaching would suffice, but it doesn't sound like it. Jennifer talked about using our talents somewhere and our service being meaningful to our community."

"Why, Dad?" Jayden piped in.

"I'm not sure, but Michael thinks she's saying it out of guilt."

"Why?" Jayden asked again.

"Michael has had some bad experiences, son. And he's also a bit of a skeptic."

"What's a septic?" Jayden asked.

Michael spit out his drink a little, and Emily bit her lip trying not to laugh hysterically.

"Not sep-tic, son. Skep-tic. It's somebody who sees the bad stuff easier than they see the good stuff," Chris said before adding, "It's just how he's unique."

Emily jumped in. "What do you think Jennifer's reason is for assigning this to you guys?"

Chris thought for a moment. "I think she feels that we've been very fortunate as a company and as individuals. And this is our way to contribute to making our community better for others." Chris recognized he was gaining some clarity from his family's questions as Jayden asked "Why?" three more times.

While Jayden's incessant questions sometimes produced weariness and frustration, this time the questions and their corresponding answers seemed helpful.

Chris began to make mental notes about some bigger questions in need of answers.

"Why am I not excited about this?" he wondered silently as he reached for another serving of veggies. "Is it because I can't think of a community issue that I especially care about? If so, does that mean I'm just not a very giving or caring person?"

He considered the alternative. "Or am I not excited because I don't have much free time, and another aspect of my life may have to suffer if I get involved with something new?"

All these questions were still rolling around in his mind throughout their dinner conversation when Chris suddenly remembered a distant memory.

When he was 15 years old, his parents had made him accompany them to a Friday night event. It was in a big conference room at a plush hotel, and there were many dressed up "old people." He remembered having to wear a tie, and he had missed going out with his friends. Chris had harbored a bad attitude about going, and it wasn't much better when he got there. But his dad had told him the event was important to them and "someday" he might reflect on it.

"I guess today's the day," he thought, recalling how after several boring speeches, rubbery chicken, green beans, and stale rolls, his parents had received an award for their service to a local literacy nonprofit. He didn't like being there, but seeing them win this honor did make him a little proud of his parents, although he would never have let them know that back then. He hadn't paid much attention through the years to the details of what his parents did in their spare time.

In his current stage of life at the start of his career in a new city with a young wife and son, serving in the community wasn't a priority or even a consideration until now. Frankly, Chris wasn't eager to add another "must do" to his already long list of tasks to prioritize. He already struggled to juggle work, home, and hobbies and couldn't picture having to add anything more.

Chris's mind was full, and not in a good way. "I wonder how my parents handled it all," Chris reflected quietly as he took another bite of dinner. "They obviously were giving back when I was a kid. They both had full-time jobs with three kids at home. I only have one."

Chris wondered how involved his parents were in the community and what roles they served. How did they manage their busy schedules?

"I just don't get it," Chris continued in his internal dialogue with himself. "Maybe I'm not as organized or committed as they were. Or, maybe they were just more passionate about helping others than I am." He was not sure he was passionate enough about any particular cause to warrant the work that would likely be involved in meeting Jennifer's requirements.

Emily could tell Chris was deep in his own thoughts, so she turned and visited with Jayden as they finished eating.

That night as Chris settled into bed after reading Jayden a bedtime story, his mind drifted back to his wife's questions about the role he was most interested in and what issue in their community he wanted to address. He hadn't been able to answer her because he wasn't sure. He wasn't even sure that he wanted to "address an issue" at all. But something else Jennifer said kept ringing in his ears.

"While this initiative was focused on giving back, we will all receive benefits," she had said.

"What does she mean by 'benefits'?" Chris had thought at the time.

As if to answer his question, Jennifer had followed up with a personal story as an example. "Early in my career, I served on a board. And that experience allowed me to test some of the leadership lessons I had received at work in a different environment. It was a pivotal moment in my leadership journey." Jennifer then explained how Sharp Edge likewise wanted to take the leadership lessons that had been instilled in their team and use them to improve their community.

As Chris stared at the ceiling, he wondered if perhaps his parents would be willing to answer some of his questions about what board service looked like. He would call them soon, but not tonight. Hopefully, sleep would take over and maybe he would have a better perspective in the morning.

◆ ◆ ◆

PERSONAL REFLECTION QUESTIONS FOR BOARD MEMBERS

Ask yourself the following questions and journal key points:

» Prior to becoming a board member, what was your perception of board service?

» What and/or who shaped your perception of board service?

» Would you recommend that others participate in board service? Why or why not?

» What leadership lessons have you learned by serving on a board?

» What leadership lessons have you learned at work that could benefit a board?

GROUP DISCUSSION QUESTIONS FOR BOARD MEMBERS

With a group of other board members, discuss the following questions and note key points:

» Why did you first join a board?

» How would you feel about a board member joining the board only because they were "required" to serve?

» How many boards have you served on? What would motivate you to serve on additional boards in the future?

» What is your company's view of serving alongside a nonprofit?

» What would you like your company's view of serving alongside a nonprofit to be? Why?

SUGGESTED ACTIONS FOR BOARD MEMBERS

» **Bronze:** Share with a colleague at work about your service on the board.

» **Silver:** Discuss your board service with friends, encouraging them to find a place to serve if they aren't doing so already.

» **Gold:** Create a vision for corporate community engagement for your company, no matter the size.

Two

Where to Go from Here?

WHEN CHRIS RETURNED TO work on Monday, the day was full of deadlines and tasks. He didn't give much attention to this "give back to the community initiative," as everyone was calling it. But he knew Jennifer was serious about it, so he couldn't put the issue aside for long.

On Tuesday he started to do some research online to better his understanding of the community needs and the nonprofits currently meeting those concerns.

Chris had so much to learn before he could even begin deciding how he would serve his community. He had heard the term "board of directors" before the Friday meeting, but he wasn't sure what that entailed. The role of a board member was top on his list for discovery.

After reading a few boring articles about boards, Chris was not feeling more enthusiastic or convinced that serving on one was something he ever wanted to do.

"I wonder what the other supervisors around here are doing and if they are as confused as I am?" Chris mused.

After grabbing his first Coke Zero of the day from the break room, he ran into Preston in the hall and took the opportunity to strike up a conversation with him. "When you have a moment, let's sit down and talk about this give back to the community thing," Chris said to him.

"No time like the present," Preston responded, walking into Chris's office and plopping down in the chair closest to the door.

Preston jumped in, apparently having more insight regarding Austin's problems than Chris had. "There are the regular issues with traffic congestion, transportation, and affordable housing. But you know hunger, homelessness, education, and mental illness are also very real problems. Plus, with all the growth, there are environmental concerns all around the Hill Country... things like water conservation and quality, endangered animals, and I'm sure dozens of other effects from losing all our green space."

Preston continued explaining that he thought one of the most ignored issues was the human trafficking taking place along I-35.

"Can you imagine that is happening right here where we drive every day? My friend was scheduled to have surgery yesterday, but he couldn't even have it because there was a lack of blood supply. Did you know that?" Preston didn't take a breath before adding, "And what about all the stray animals? It's hard to decide, Chris. I can't choose just one issue that I'm passionate about when there are so many big issues facing us. Where do we even start?"

Chris was overwhelmed, but not for the same reason as

Preston. Chris had been completely unaware of the multitude of problems and felt inadequate to help solve any of them.

"Take a deep breath," he said to himself as Preston waited for his response. What is the best way to begin solving any problem? Chris smiled as he remembered a corny saying that his grandpa used to say to him.

"How do you eat an elephant, Preston?" Chris suddenly asked.

"Huh? What do you mean?" Preston questioned, anticipating the punch line.

"One bite at a time," Chris replied. "That's what my grandpa used to say. Let's try just focusing on one thing first and see where that takes us. The first issue you mentioned was traffic congestion. Let's find out more about that one."

Chris turned and started typing on his computer, looking for nonprofit organizations that were already positively impacting traffic issues in Austin. He questioned how effective their efforts could possibly be, especially considering that more people flocked to Austin from all over the country every year.

"It looks like there are quite a number of local and national organizations addressing traffic," Chris said, pointing to the screen.

"Yeah, but does it say what they do?" Preston inquired.

"Well, it looks like this one is focused on a variety of solutions," Chris suggested, clicking on a link. He read aloud from the website about increasing car-pooling, making public transportation more accessible, and advocating for more remote working.

"That sounds interesting," Preston replied. "Can you tell if they are looking for volunteers?"

"I don't see anything here, but maybe check their LinkedIn or Facebook page later," Chris said.

"That's a great idea! Thanks for talking this through a little, Chris. I'm feeling better." Preston looked at his phone. "Oh, man. I have another meeting. I have to run. I'll take another bite out of that elephant later." Preston, the eternal optimist, headed out the door to his next meeting.

"Well, I'm glad that was at least helpful to Preston," Chris thought. Frustrated, he decided to hold off researching more topics for now and went back to learning more about boards and their role in nonprofit organizations. A fastidious planner, Chris scheduled 15 minutes on his calendar each day for the rest of the week to continue his research.

He ended the week feeling more informed on the community's needs and what was being done to meet them. But he was no closer to discovering what his role should be. Also, he still wasn't convinced that he wanted to take on any role at all. Then he remembered that it wasn't an optional activity!

As he headed to the parking garage on Friday afternoon, his thoughts were back to square one. "What could one man do anyway?" he asked himself, unsure he could fulfill Jennifer's mandate without being overwhelmed.

Those thoughts didn't stay idle long, as he had a date night with Emily, and he was eager to get her take on all of it. Once they settled into a table at Clay Pit, their favorite contemporary Indian cuisine restaurant, Chris began to share some of the details he had uncovered during his research. They talked a lot about what he had learned so far. He shared with Emily how he had always assumed some areas needed help with food and other necessities but hadn't given it much thought beyond that.

He was surprised to find so many organizations even existed in Austin, including ones providing foster care support, caring for victims of sex trafficking, and assisting children whose parents were in prison.

Emily listened thoughtfully and then repeated a question she'd asked once before. "Christopher, is there a problem that's resonated with you? Something you think you would be passionate enough about to invest in?"

Despite all his research, Chris was still unable to answer her.

"No, and that's the problem. While they all seem important, nothing jumps out at me. I'm kind of at an impasse," Chris confessed.

His mind quickly jumped to the last time he went hiking and climbing in Colorado. He eventually came to a real impasse then. But he had paused, looked at his surroundings, studied his map, and came up with a new course of action to reach the peak. If only it was that easy this time.

Emily encouraged Chris, "Keep your eyes, heart, and mind open, and I bet one issue will rise to the top."

Chris asked her to repeat what she just said, and she did so. He could only hope Emily was right.

◆

Chris woke up early on Saturday, irritated that he couldn't sleep late on the weekend. It was the one week of the fall when their team had a bye, which meant there was no soccer game scheduled and he could sleep in. But the habit of waking up early was too ingrained in him. Instead of lying in bed, he decided to get up and start moving. Emily didn't appear as if she was getting up anytime soon. He stopped by to check on Jayden, who was spooning with a stuffed animal and deep in sleep.

After tossing a K-cup in the Keurig, hitting the largest serving, and pouring the hot, steaming chai tea into a travel mug, he headed out the door and hopped into his F-150 truck. The truck wasn't necessary for his lifestyle or his work, but after a few years in the Lone Star State, it seemed like the natural purchase for him. He turned up the music and paid careful attention to his surroundings. For a while, he drove around town, curious to follow Emily's suggestion and see if any community issues popped to the top of his list. He still had some time to decide, but he was getting nowhere fast.

Over an hour later, he pulled back in his driveway. "That was a waste of time," he concluded. "There's got to be a better way to figure this out." But, not today. Today he would focus on enjoying time with Emily and Jayden. "It can wait until Monday," he told himself. Or so he thought.

By this time, Emily and Jayden were up and raring to go. They often drove to the farmer's market on Saturdays, and that was exactly what Emily had in mind for the day. Emily liked to buy fresh produce, and Jayden enjoyed petting the dogs and trying the homemade ice cream.

The three of them pulled into the parking lot and noticed an extra row of tents and tables to the side of the market.

"What do you think is going on there?" Emily asked.

"I'm not sure. Maybe there are more vendors than usual today," Chris replied.

As they made their way over to the tent area, they realized the extra tents were not selling anything. Instead, each table was hosted by various nonprofit organizations to spread the word about their causes and services. Chris vaguely remembered seeing this kind of emphasis at the farmer's market before, but he had always intentionally skipped over it. This time, he was their target audience!

Chris was a bit disappointed by his bad luck since he'd hoped for a distraction from the ongoing dialogue in his head. However, he was here and knew that he should take advantage of talking with some organizations.

Emily patiently nudged him in that direction. "Go ahead and look around. Jayden wants ice cream anyway, so I'll take him and meet up with you in a few."

Chris sighed deeply and set off toward a brightly decorated table, while Emily and Jayden scooted off to greet an adorable golden retriever puppy that had just arrived.

Forty-five minutes later, they all came away from the market with something. Jayden got his puppy fix and some ice cream. Emily found fresh kale and broccoli. And Chris got to hear the pitches of more nonprofits than he realized existed in Austin, even though hundreds more were not represented at the market.

As they headed for the truck, Emily asked, "So?"

"It was kind of exhausting. They all talk a good game about what they're doing and the needs, but I'm no closer to knowing where I'm headed."

"Did you see that Great Dane, Dad?" Jayden chimed in. "He was bigger than my playground!"

Chris gave an enthusiastically positive response, but he was distracted. He didn't know where to go from here. "Should I volunteer first?" he wondered. "Or do I fill out an application?"

Jayden was still talking about all the dogs he saw when Chris rejoined his family's conversation.

◆

Sunday afternoon rolled around, and Chris decided this was a good time to call his parents to get their perspective.

"Christopher, so good to hear your voice. Let me get your dad on the phone," his mom began.

The phone went dead.

Chris had come to expect this. About a quarter of the time, he would get disconnected at some point in the conversation with his parents. He just grinned, shook his head, and redialed as usual. His dad picked up this time, and his mom joined from another room. They proceeded with updates on recent visits to doctors, the weather, and inquired about Jayden's school accomplishments.

Chris changed the direction of the conversation. "I want to pick your brain on something. My company is mandating that everyone in management be more engaged in the community. I'm starting to wonder about serving on a board, and…"

His dad cut him off. "That's one of the greatest things I ever did, Christopher! You know the tree in the backyard, the one we planted when you were nine?"

His dad didn't wait for an answer.

"You know how you feel when Jayden sits under that tree on a hot day? Multiply that exponentially, and that's how I feel when I think about Straight from Nature and the work they're doing in our community. We're alleviating food deserts in our community, son!"

Straight from Nature was the name of one of the food banks where his parents currently served near their home in

Bakersfield, California. Their efforts included partnering with local farmers and ranchers to establish processes for the safe delivery of fresh vegetables and meats directly to families. The organization also partnered with local church food pantries, schools, and daycares to educate parents and caregivers on the importance of healthy eating.

His mom jumped in and added, "I agree with your dad. I've had great experiences on boards, and I've had some challenging ones. They're all meaningful, but not always enjoyable."

Chris listened, mostly because he could not get a word in! His parents recalled their past and present experiences working with nonprofit organizations in many capacities. Chris had no idea how involved his parents had been and still were. He was most surprised at how meaningful their service had been. The passion in their voices was inspiring as they jumped from story to story of improving the health and well-being of needy families. Their testimony contradicted the cynical take shared by Michael during last week's run.

After the conversation with his parents, Chris found himself a little more enthused about the idea of serving on a board. "Thanks so much for sharing such vivid details of your experiences with me. I had no idea how impactful your volunteer work had been in your lives," he told them. They talked a little more about family and upcoming plans before ending the call.

As he hung up, he once again remembered Jennifer telling the management team how much they would also benefit from their volunteer work. Chris couldn't imagine that happening, but his parents seemed to agree with her. He decided he wanted to ask Jennifer what she meant, and since he didn't want to lose momentum or chicken out, he texted her right then.

> **Can we meet on Monday morning?
> I want to talk to you about this
> community engagement emphasis.**

He pushed "send" and then reconsidered how his text might be interpreted, so he added:

> **I'm excited!**

and hit "send" again.

An hour went by, and Chris received a response from Jennifer.

> **That's funny. I already typed an
> email to you, but I delayed the
> delivery until Monday. I want
> you to join the board where I'm
> serving...if you're interested in
> the cause. Can't do Monday,
> but we'll talk this week. Have a
> great weekend with your family.**

Jennifer was good about protecting family time when possible, so he wasn't surprised that she delayed her email. She and her husband, James, had three kids, and two of them were already out of the house. "How does she balance it all?" Chris speculated silently.

He wished he could get an answer to his questions now, especially since Jennifer could not meet on Monday. But he simply responded:

> **Sounds good. Thanks!**

The curiosity was killing him. He wondered what organization Jennifer had in mind (she served with a few) and, more importantly, why she had thought of him to join the board.

◆

The next week, Chris walked into Jennifer's office, handed her a coffee with a little cream, and asked, "Why me?"

Jennifer chuckled and said, "Is there sugar in it?" pointing to her cup.

"Of course not!" Chris quipped back. He'd learned the hard way how Jennifer liked her coffee: with cream only, and not much cream at that.

"First, I want to share a little about the organization I thought you might like and explain the mission. We can see if it's one that you're interested in being a part of. If it is, then we'll go from there, and I'll answer your question. It's Travis County Cares, TCC for short. Have you ever heard of it?"

Chris shook his head, signaling that he hadn't.

Jennifer continued, "TCC's mission is to empower people to overcome hardship and re-enter our community as independent, productive citizens. We work directly with the homeless population to provide connections to food, shelter, and necessities first. And then we partner with other agencies to address longer-term needs such as education, mental health, stable housing, and employment."

Chris thought it interesting how Jennifer used "we."

She took a swig of coffee and watched for his reaction, but didn't get much to work with. So she circled back around to Chris's question about why she had selected him.

"I can't read if you are interested or not, but I'll go ahead and address your initial question. Why you? Well, we use a board matrix to make decisions about who we want to serve." A board matrix, she explained, is a tool for charting the skills, characteristics, demographics, and contacts the various board members possess. "Ideally, before recruiting new members, the board will review the matrix and determine the criteria they want them to meet. A board matrix helps us see who we need now and in the future. This way, we don't have five attorneys, but nobody with any construction experience, for example. Let me pull up the matrix on my screen."

As Chris looked at the gigantic monitor affixed on her wall, he noticed initials distinguished each TCC board member and details like age range, gender, ethnicity, and where each member lived in the community. He also saw when their board terms would end and their specific skill sets, including public relations, accounting, and strategic planning. There was also a line about their board service experience.

"There's a whole lot more that goes into this than I thought," Chris stated. "So, back to my original question. Why me?"

"Oh, yes. I went down a rabbit trail, didn't I? As you can see, the board is a little light on the representation of people in their 30s, and several of our incoming candidates were females. So, from a demographic perspective, you were a fit. Also, during this season, we need people who are great relationally and good communicators. We want members who can go to a meeting in the community, for example, and represent TCC well."

Sharp Edge had invested in Chris by sending him to several Dale Carnegie courses where he learned many tips and techniques on leadership, sales—and most recently—presenting in front of groups. He was a gifted speaker.

"I've seen you present," Jennifer continued, "and it is certainly a strength. I thought those skills could be helpful, based on the current needs of the organization."

That all made sense to Chris, and he held back a grin, appreciating that a top leader at Sharp Edge would consider him so useful.

Jennifer added, "So I want you to think about it for a few days, and then get back to me with a decision." Chris was thankful to hear he had some time to think.

He walked a little taller as he went back to his office. Some might even say he strutted. He was still curious about the board matrix concept, so he hung up his jacket, fixed his most recently acquired polka-dotted pocket square, sat down at his desk, and set a timer on his phone for 15 minutes. He searched online for "board matrix." He saw that many nonprofit organizations used a board matrix to help select new members for service. It certainly resonated with Chris that boards would seek diversity to draw on several unique perspectives. He'd used something similar when hiring for his team at Sharp Edge. Not everyone was entirely sold on using a board matrix this way, however. While many think it's a great tool to build a well-rounded, high-functioning power team, Chris saw that some experts had a word of caution. It had to be used specific to the needs of the organization, not just for the sake of having diversity. If Chris agreed to serve with TCC, he determined to learn more about their current and future goals.

As he neared the end of his allotted study time, Chris realized that what he'd learned could also help him be a better hiring manager in the future. He was starting to see a glimmer of what Jennifer was talking about when she said this board thing would result in benefits for both parties. It'd be better for Austin and better for Sharp Edge Marketing.

◆

"Listen to this!" Chris said to Emily as he walked in the front door after work. "Jennifer asked me to serve on a board that she's on. They do something to help the homeless."

"Is it TCC?" Emily asked, watching Chris hang up his jacket as she put the finishing touches on dinner.

"Travis County Cares! Yes, that's it. How do you know about it?"

"I do spin class with a woman who works there. Her name is Michelle, and I really like her and the way she cares about the homeless. She's told a few of us some stories about their work, and it sounds exciting! That's crazy that she works for the same organization that Jennifer is involved with," Emily noted, pulling some salad out of the fridge.

"Small world!" Chris said, pleased to hear that Emily thought so highly of TCC already.

"Last week, Michelle shared about their big annual event and some inspiring guest speaker who delivered the keynote." Emily recalled that the speaker was one of TCC's former clients with a particularly difficult past who overcame homelessness and drug addiction to become a high school history teacher.

"Michelle started crying while telling us this story. Before long, we were all crying...except Bob, of course," Emily said.

Chris laughed. Bob was one of the only guys in Emily's class, and the women considered him emotionally cold.

"What else do you know about TCC?" Chris wanted to

know.

"Well, a while back, I asked Michelle how they're funded," Emily continued. "She said some money comes from the government, but much of it comes from private donations and foundations."

"Jennifer shared that with me, too," Chris added. "She also said that each board member is asked to contribute financially."

Emily looked up suddenly.

"No specific dollar amount is required," Chris clarified. "It's just an amount that fits within their personal family budget. I guess we will need to talk about that if I join."

Emily agreed that they would need to sit down and discuss a reasonable amount to commit to financially. In a few minutes, the three of them were sitting down to eat dinner.

◆

The following day, Jennifer sent Chris a text.

Pop by my office if you can. I'd like to introduce you to someone.

As Chris walked into Jennifer's office, a casually dressed woman who appeared to be about twice his age stood up and greeted him with a smile.

"Chris, I want to introduce you to Michelle. She's our fabulous executive director at TCC," Jennifer stated with enthusiasm.

Chris paused, surprised that the mental image he'd created of the friend from Emily's spin class didn't match up with reality at all. "Well, it's great to meet you, Michelle! Jennifer has certainly been bragging about you," Chris began. "And, I believe you know my wife, Emily."

Michelle tilted her head sideways, trying to make the connection.

"From spin class..."

"That's the context clue I needed! I love that gal! She's a treat—and a beast on the bike!"

"I'm sure!" Chris replied.

Jennifer, Michelle, and Chris talked about TCC a little more and even settled on a date for Chris to come by and volunteer a few hours. Then Chris excused himself to get back to work.

He found the dialogue helpful, and it made him think he might have finally found his place in the community. Chris smiled and thought, "This may actually be fun." He wouldn't recognize it for many years to come, but he had just experienced a significant turning point in his life.

◆ ◆ ◆

PERSONAL REFLECTION QUESTIONS FOR BOARD MEMBERS

Ask yourself the following questions and journal key points:

» How important is a board member's personal passion regarding a cause?

» What needs in your community does your nonprofit serve?

» What three people can you identify who are passionate about a need/issue but are not currently serving a nonprofit organization?

» What five words/phrases describe your perspective about board service?

» How are you uniquely equipped to add value to the nonprofit you serve?

GROUP DISCUSSION QUESTIONS FOR BOARD MEMBERS

With a group of other board members, discuss the following questions and note key points:

» Are we clear on our goals for the year and the next few years? Explain.

» How do we fare at recruiting great board members on a scale of 1-10 (10 being the best)? Why?

» What can we do in the next year to recruit future talent for the board?

» If you use a board matrix to determine board needs: What elements are missing currently or will be missing in the next year?

» If you **don't** use a board matrix to determine board needs: What are the pros and cons of creating and using a board matrix to guide future recruitment?

» What skills/knowledge/strengths are we likely to need on the board for the coming year (considering our goals)?

Suggested Actions for Board Members

» **Bronze:** Familiarize yourself with the various programs of your nonprofit.

» **Silver:** After familiarizing yourself with your nonprofit's programs, seek to understand what other organizations are doing similar or overlapping work.

» **Gold:** Research why these programs are necessary for the population your organization serves. What is the community's history with each issue?

THREE

Let the Onboarding Begin

As soon as he walked into the TCC facility, Chris could feel the energy. A woman who must have been in her 70s greeted him.

"Hello! I'm Betty," she said enthusiastically.

Chris introduced himself and told Betty he was there to volunteer.

"Well, welcome to TCC!" she said. "Thanks for coming today. Let me show you around. I've been volunteering here for four years, and one of my favorite tasks is meeting new volunteers and getting them excited about the amazing work going on here." Betty walked Chris around the downtown facility, introducing him to other volunteers and staff members.

"This is Mikey," Betty said as she introduced Chris to a man who looked like a modern version of Santa Claus. He was a muscular, burly guy with a happy smile and a snow-white beard. Chris wasn't quite close enough to make out the beautifully detailed full sleeve tattoos, but he could tell they were quite a piece of art. "Mikey heads up food distribution, both in our dining area and on the streets."

"How many people do you serve a day, Mikey?" Chris asked.

"Well, 287 meals were served in our dining room at lunchtime today. And we distributed another 92 meals outside the walls. That's close to average."

"That's a remarkable number, and I'm also impressed you know your facts," Chris replied.

"This is what I do! It's my life, and I love it," Mikey shared with a big smile.

Chris enjoyed seeing everyone in action as Betty showed him around.

After the tour, Chris spent time sorting donated winter items such as coats, gloves, hats, and blankets. These would be distributed to various locations with high populations of homeless people. Though the winter weather had been mild thus far, it wasn't unusual for January and February, and sometimes even March, to bring a cold blast from the Rockies to the Hill Country of Texas.

As Chris went through the pile of items alongside a college student volunteer from the University of Texas, he felt a sense of pride doing something positive like this for his community. So much of his job with Sharp Edge was in the communication realm. And while he enjoyed his work and believed those strengths could benefit a nonprofit organization like TCC, he also enjoyed contributing in a tactical, hands-on way.

Chris wondered if Emily and Jayden would be interested in joining him to volunteer one weekend. He thought back to his childhood as he worked. It would be nice for Jayden to experience the joy of helping others. And it would give his son some perspective of life beyond the bubble of his comfortable suburban neighborhood. Chris made a mental note to mention it to Emily over dinner that evening.

He told the college student working with him that he might bring his family with him next time. "My parents were very involved in giving back to the community, but they never involved me," Chris explained. Realistically, they may have invited Chris, but he wasn't interested then. Or they may have assumed he would have copped an attitude. "I did have a bit of insolence," Chris recalled to himself.

The shy UT student just smiled, but Chris made a second mental note to find out more the next time he talked to his parents.

◆

On the first day of January, Chris officially joined the board of TCC, and Jennifer became the board chair. Eager to learn all he could, Chris scheduled a time with her to discuss the best way to get up to speed. He wanted to know what he should do to start his service, promising himself that he would continue his hands-on experience at TCC and not just be in the board room.

Jennifer expressed excitement at Chris's enthusiasm. "I appreciate your taking the initiative to meet. What's on your mind?"

"I know you have expectations, and there's so much for me to learn about TCC and what a board member even does. So what should my first 90 days look like?"

"Listen, Chris," she warned him, keenly aware that Chris was the consummate planner. "You need to know upfront that you're not going to get the same level of onboarding at TCC as you did at Sharp Edge. When I started on the board, there was nothing for new board members. Nothing! However, that's all changed. Between Michelle's experience and some things I've brought over from Sharp Edge, you'll get more information than any other new board member ever had. The upcoming board retreat will also give our members a greater understanding of TCC and help us harness our board's talent. But you'll still want to do some research yourself. Michelle gave you dates for the onboarding, board meetings, training, and the retreat, right? Let me tell you something, you won't want to miss that retreat! It's a full day, but you'll glean so much and be fired up afterward."

Chris nodded affirmatively.

Jennifer then suggested that Chris study the homeless problem in Austin, paying careful attention to what was already being done to help. "An onboarding training session will be scheduled soon for all our new board members," Jennifer said. "But if you want to hit the ground running, why don't you set a date to tour TCC?"

"Actually, I already did that," Chris said. "I signed up to volunteer back in November, and Betty gave me a tour."

"Really?" Jennifer asked, her eyes wide with surprise.

"Yes, why do you look so shocked?"

"Well, I'm just pleasantly surprised that you took such initiative when your board position hadn't even started yet."

Chris was glad his boss was proud of him, and he was even

happier that he'd seen TCC in action for himself because it put him that much ahead for his first upcoming board meeting.

◆

Chris was nervous but ready when the initial onboarding session rolled around. He showed up about 10 minutes early and settled into a seat. The room was full, but he didn't recognize anyone other than Jennifer, who was busy with last-minute preparations, and Michelle, the executive director.

"Hi, I'm Chris," he stated to a woman sitting across from him.

"Hello, I'm Susan. Are you also a new board member?" she asked, but seemed preoccupied with her phone.

"I am," Chris responded.

Susan stared at her phone without replying. He wasn't sure what to say or ask next, so he was relieved when the executive director began the meeting by welcoming the four new board members, including Chris.

Juan was a vibrant, smiling man who stood quite a bit taller than Chris and had shoulders just as broad as his smile. Susan's dated pantsuit reminded Chris of a handler's dress code straight out of the Westminster Kennel Club Dog Show. She forced a smile when introduced, keeping her phone in her hand and avoiding handshakes. LaShonda was a 30-something sharply dressed woman who exuded confidence and warmth equally. She looked familiar, but Chris had no idea where he would have met her. Chris was immediately drawn to Juan and LaShonda as people he would like to know better. His mom had always told him, "You will become more and more like the people you surround yourself with." He could tell just by their pleasant demeanor that they would be nice to be around. Chris even thought of inviting Juan and LaShonda and their spouses over for dinner. He wasn't so sure about Susan. He berated himself for judging her so quickly, while simultaneously noting that his instincts about people were often right.

"Thanks so much for serving at TCC! In a minute, we'll each introduce ourselves and share why we chose to serve. But, before we do, it's time for a pop quiz!" Michelle's tone was energetic and friendly, matching Emily's stories about her from spin class.

The fact that Emily liked Michelle eased Chris's nerves, as he trusted her gut feel on people. She also had a knack for reading people and sensing their honesty and integrity.

The quiz included a fill-in-the-blank on the organization's mission, their annual budget, the level of need regarding area homeless, the primary areas of TCC's strategic plan, and their four key programs. Chris didn't see those questions coming and had a hard time answering the quiz.

While Chris had invested a lot of research on homelessness in Travis County and the various organizations tackling the issue, he hadn't done detailed research on the TCC website. Most of what he knew included general details provided through his discussions with Jennifer and his little time volunteering and touring.

Michelle sat down and had a playful grin on her face as she read out the answers. The exercise did exactly what she was hoping; it helped her understand what the board already knew (and didn't know) about the organization and the homeless population in Travis County.

Afterwards, Michelle jumped up from her seat and said, "It's time for some speed dating, minus the dating. I want you to get to know your fellow new board members. What questions might be good to ask? This isn't rhetorical, by the way!" The group gave several ideas while Michelle wrote them on a flipchart. The list included:

- Have you served on other boards before?

- Why did you agree to join the TCC board?

- What expertise do you bring to the organization?

- Do you have a personal connection to homelessness? If yes, what is it?

Michelle encouraged and redirected the group a little as they discussed these suggestions. "Those are good. What personal questions would you also like to ask your colleagues?"

Juan, Susan, Chris, and LaShonda added a few personal questions and ideas to the growing list, including:

- What would you like us to know about your family?

- What do you love about your work?

- What's the biggest challenge you have overcome?

- How would your family or friends describe you?

"Whoa!" Juan said, looking over the list. "I guess we're really going to get to know each other!"

When it was time to begin the "speed dating" round, Chris was ready. He liked the idea of connecting with those he'd be serving with, and he jumped right in.

"Each of you will rotate to meet the other new members," Michelle explained. "Take turns introducing yourselves, making sure you answer all of the questions I wrote on the flipchart. Juan, why don't you and Chris partner and LaShonda and Susan pair up for the first round?"

Chris pointed his chair in the direction of Juan, got his pen ready to take some notes, and asked, "Are you up for going first?"

"Sure," Juan replied somewhat shyly, and he began to share about himself.

"Well, I'm Juan. I've never served on a board before, but my neighbor is on staff here at TCC as the office manager. She encouraged me to consider a position on the board because of my background. I recently took over as general manager of my family's construction and painting business that my grandfather started 51 years ago when he first moved to the United States. My dad had been managing the business for the last 25 years or so, but he decided it was time to step out after having some health issues. I was surprised when my dad asked me to take over. I didn't feel ready for so much responsibility, much less make such a big move with my family. We were living in Mexico City when my dad visited and asked me to consider a move to Austin. I was working for my wife's booming interior design company and we already felt overwhelmed. But, after considering the offer fully, we decided that I would take the job, split our time between the two cities, and move the boys to schools in Austin. So here I am. The business has 18 employees, and they are all depending on me. It's a lot of pressure! Oh, and I have been married to my wife, Yvette, for 10 years. We have three sons who are eight, five, and one."

"Three kids under 10, a big career move, and living in two cities. You have a lot going on!" Chris observed. "How do you unwind during the free time you do have?"

"Well, I don't have a lot of that these days, but I coach my boys' soccer teams. I hope I can continue to juggle it all."

Chris could relate to that dilemma.

"Okay, I guess it's your turn," Juan prompted.

Chris introduced himself and stole a look at the flipchart at the front of the room to remember all the questions he was supposed to answer. Mostly he felt that he rambled and couldn't clearly verbalize what made him decide to join the board. Perhaps that was because it still wasn't clear in his own mind.

Juan nodded while Chris talked, but didn't ask any follow-up questions, so Chris's turn ended quickly. They sat quietly for a few minutes, and Chris took a few more notes. Juan appeared to be about 30 years old and wore cowboy boots and a ball cap that sported his company logo. Chris also jotted down a few things they shared in common. Both had sons, and both coached soccer. It seemed quite easy to strike up a conversation with Juan.

Michelle asked them all to rotate clockwise, so Chris moved around the table to meet LaShonda. Without hesitation, LaShonda began her introduction.

"Hi, Chris! I am not a Texan by birth, but I got here as soon as I could." Chris chuckled at the Texas humor and relaxed a bit. It sounded as if LaShonda's spiel would be entertaining, so Chris leaned back in his chair to enjoy it.

"I grew up in the Northeast, mostly outside of Albany, New York. Eight years ago, my world turned upside down when my husband and I divorced. It was devastating. I didn't see it coming. We never had any children, so I felt especially alone."

Chris was surprised that LaShonda would share so much personal information with strangers but was drawn into her story at the same time. LaShonda continued, "Since I was a child, I dreamed of going to law school and decided that perhaps it was time to fulfill that dream. That brought me to St. Mary's School of Law in San Antonio. After a few years of hard work, I graduated with top honors in my class. I always assumed I would head back north, but before graduation, I was offered a great job as an attorney for The University of Texas. So, I moved here four years ago, met the man of my dreams, and remarried about a year later. I love my life in Austin. I love the culture, the food, the music, and running along Barton Creek and Lady Bird Lake."

Chris interrupted. "That's where I've seen you! It was driving me crazy. I'm a runner, too. Go ahead."

She nodded and continued, "I never, never would have imagined that I would have the job and relationship of my dreams, especially in Texas! I have fallen in love with Texas, minus August, and the many wonderful things that have happened since moving here, though I still miss my family."

Then LaShonda shared a story that brought the real purpose of TCC into focus. "The reality of being so far away hit me especially hard recently. My brother Ron, who was struggling with mental illness and living on the streets in Brooklyn, died from pneumonia. Our family hadn't heard from him in months and didn't even know that he was homeless. It broke my heart to know that Ron was out there alone. We could have been with him. We could have helped get him medical care. But instead, he was alone and too sick by the time he arrived at the hospital. To honor him, I decided to find an organization in Austin serving people like my brother. Those men and women out there are someone's brother or sister, and son or daughter. They need someone. They need us."

Chris was quiet for a while, and he let the weight of the story linger. It was obvious that LaShonda had a genuinely soft and caring heart for the mentally ill and homeless.

"I'm so sorry to hear about the loss of your brother. That must have been devastating," Chris said sympathetically.

"Yes, it absolutely was, but I know there is a plan for me through this tragedy. And I want to take my grief and make it a light to others."

Chris was humbled by LaShonda's perspective and felt a bit child-like as he began his introduction. "Well, that's tough to follow! You are very inspiring. I don't have much of a story to tell, so I guess I'll just tell you some facts about me."

Chris methodically went down the list of questions, answering each one and then moving to the next. Despite his less-than-interesting presentation, LaShonda smiled and followed up on certain answers. They chatted easily until Michelle called "time" to make the final switch of partners.

Chris moved toward Susan, and she asked if he wanted to go first.

"Sure! I've learned so much about everyone. This was such a good idea," Chris began. Feeling a bit more comfortable with the flow of his introduction, Chris moved from point to point. As soon as he finished talking, Susan started sharing her own story without asking anything additional about him.

"I'm Susan, and I was born and raised here in Austin. I

know, that seems to be more and more rare these days. I've been married to my husband, Tom, for 34 years. We have three adult children. I have served on many boards over the years, maybe a dozen or more. I especially enjoy the camaraderie and fellowship of it all. My greatest strengths are communication, details, listening, and organization—all of which boards seem to need. I learned about TCC through some volunteer work I did with Habitat for Humanity doing home repairs. It was there that I met a board member of TCC who sparked my interest in this organization. And here I am."

Chris made some notes but didn't have a lot to write. Susan hadn't shared much about herself beyond some surface-level details, and what she did share sounded dry and rehearsed. There wasn't anything particularly off-putting to Chris, but the way that she said it didn't seem genuine for some reason. Chris decided to try to get to know her better.

"Wow, you have a lot of experience working with nonprofits! I'm sure I will have a ton to learn from you. What advice do you have for someone like me who hasn't ever worked with a nonprofit before?" Chris asked.

"Well, I'm not sure how to answer that. What kind of advice are you looking for exactly?" Susan snapped a bit harshly.

"I mean, I'm not looking for anything specific," Chris answered sheepishly. He was surprised that his friendly question had garnered such a strange response.

"Oh, okay. I guess I would just say to go into this eyes wide open. Don't believe everything you hear," Susan responded flatly. "I have been participating on boards for a long time, and there's always more going on than what you can see."

Chris had no idea what Susan was referring to, but he

decided he didn't want to know. "Okay, thanks," he responded and decided to leave it at that. Either Susan had come across some bad boards in her past, he surmised, or she was just a negative person in general. Or perhaps both. Susan didn't volunteer anything else, and Chris decided to act busy reading over his notes from the other discussions until their time was over.

Once the introductions were complete, Michelle announced it was time for a break. Chris headed to a table with snacks and drinks, still shaking his head about his ineloquent introductions. Surely the others wondered how he'd even been selected for the board! The other new board members seemed to have passion or experience or both, but Chris didn't come across as having either. To make matters worse, he recalled that Jennifer wanted him on the board because of his "great communication skills"!

◆

As they came back into the conference room after the break, Michelle stood in the front of the room, visiting with Jennifer and another person. Chris waved at Jennifer but didn't recognize the other man. Chris sat down and read a quote projected on the TV screen. It read, "Some people were born on third base and thought they hit a triple."

At that moment, Michelle stood up and asked for everyone's attention. "I want you to pair up and discuss the quote that you see on the screen," Michelle said.

Juan pointed at Chris, signifying they should pair up. Chris moved his chair to face Juan.

Chris smirked a little, pondering the words he recognized

from the legendary football coach Barry Switzer. "I think I might be guilty of that, but only for a double," he said as he pointed at the screen.

Juan nodded. "In some ways, I might be at third base. In other ways, I'm not sure I've made it to first base yet!"

They continued discussing the privileges and benefits they had received from previous generations, as well as the opportunities afforded to them. The conversation was very comfortable, and they both agreed that their grandparents, and even parents, did not have it as good as they did.

Michelle then got the attention of everyone in the room and introduced Jennifer as the current board chair. Jennifer stood up, smiled, and said, "Thank you all so much for your service to TCC and the Austin community. And, on behalf of the board, welcome! Michelle has raised the bar on onboarding our new members, and I bet your fellow board members are already jealous of what you'll experience. What you will gain in the first couple of months will be the equivalent of what we might have received over the course of our first two years! So, please join me in thanking Michelle!"

As applause erupted among the four new board members, Michelle stepped back up. Her cheeks were glowing pink, as she was not used to the public praise.

"Thank you, Jennifer, for your kind words and for challenging me to enhance our new board member onboarding training. Thank you also for the many great ideas you brought from Sharp Edge to TCC. Now, I have a special guest speaker," Michelle continued. "I don't want to share too much because you will want to hear it directly from him. So, without delay, let me introduce one of our clients and a fellow volunteer, Scott."

Scott was standing just outside the open doorway and entered the room promptly when Michelle said his name. He looked to be in his mid-forties and donned an Army veteran hat, along with jeans and a well-worn flannel shirt. Despite the casualness of his dress, Scott made a good impression. Everything was clean, his clothes fit him well, and his shirt was tucked in— hardly the commonly imagined picture of a homeless person.

"I hope that my story helps give you some perspective about the people we serve at TCC," Scott started. He took a deep breath and looked down nervously. And then he shared his story. "I grew up in Rockford, Illinois. Things were good enough when I was a kid. I wasn't sure what to do when I graduated from high school, and my dad said that I either needed to get a job and move out on my own or join the Army. So I joined the Army. It was great for me. I loved being independent and out on my own, even if I felt confined by Army living. I don't want to share much about the more difficult times I had during that time. I'll just say that after losing my hearing in one ear in an IED blast that took the life of one of my comrades, I decided it was time to plan my exit.

"I didn't want to return to the frigid winters of Illinois, so I took a Greyhound to Houston. Unfortunately, I couldn't find work when I got there, and I was very discouraged. I had gone straight from home to the Army and had never been completely on my own, even though I thought I was independent. The Army pretty much told me how to live. I had heard Austin was booming, so I hitchhiked here. Turns out, that was a bad decision, at first. I drank too much and experimented with drugs a little. I lost my motivation and couldn't find a way to climb out of the hole I was in. I was down and out. That is, until I became part of the TCC Bright Horizon program."

He went on to share that he was scheduled to graduate from the program in three months. He'd learned life skills, had a job, kept his space clean in his transitional house, and even became the "go-to cook" for the other residents.

"You want to know my nickname in the house?" Scott asked. "They call me *Mom*!" And with that, he smiled shyly and nodded to Michelle that he was finished talking.

Juan and LaShonda wiped away a couple of tears as Scott said goodbye and left the room. His story was truly inspiring. Chris had a hard time imagining having to face the challenges that Scott had overcome.

Michelle spent the next few minutes presenting various statistics about homelessness in the United States and in Austin. Chris was shocked to learn that well over 2,000 individuals experienced homelessness in Travis County on a single day. Over 1,000 of those did not have shelter. A sense of gloom settled inside the conference room, and everyone was quiet as the magnitude of the problem sunk in.

"Okay, folks, we have covered a lot of information so far, and I'm sure your heads are spinning," Michelle said, wrapping up their time. "Look around this room. These are some of the people you will be serving with, and they are all new to the board just like you. Continue getting to know each other as you learn and grow in your role. Before we dismiss, take a look back over your notes, and review the details about your peers. What a great group!"

Chris dutifully read over his notes:

Juan:

- Father of 3, married for 10 years.

- Owns a remodeling construction and paint company that employs 18 people

- Took over his business from his father

- Also lives in Mexico City some of the time where his wife has a business

- Coaches soccer

- Never served on a board before

LaShonda:

- Grew up in the Northeast

- Went to law school

- Attorney at University of Texas

- Recently married

- Likes to run around Lady Bird Lake with her new husband

- Brother was homeless and died from pneumonia in 2020

Susan:

- Married for 34 years

- 3 adult children

- Has served on about a dozen boards in the past

- Expertise is in planning and communication

- Very detail-oriented, according to her

- Distracted? Grumpy? Or both!

Chris thought as he looked up from the page, "I'm going to enjoy serving with Juan and LaShonda, and I hope I get some more time to get to know Scott, too. I should give Susan the benefit of the doubt, but there are some gaps to be filled in. I'm not sure about her."

They all had so much life experience to offer. Chris still felt underwhelmed about the value he brought to the table and wondered if others could sense his insecurities.

"We've been sitting too long. Follow me for a tour," Michelle said enthusiastically.

"Um, is it safe to leave my laptop?" Chris asked hesitantly as everyone got up from the table. He hated to ask, but he wasn't sure about the security of the area.

Michelle picked up on his conflicting feelings. "It's okay to ask. Our building, in general, is very secure. We have never had issues with things going missing, but I'll lock the door, just to be extra safe."

They toured the premises, starting on the far side of the building and worked their way back. Chris studied the clients, staff, and volunteers carefully as they walked. "It looks like people enjoy working together here, and the clients seem genuinely thankful for the services," Chris told the group between stops.

"Originally, there was a very institutional approach," Michelle added. "In recent years, even before I started at TCC, the organization has transformed the culture to have a much more caring attitude. We still have rules, because I have seen there can be a lot of abuse within the homeless population, but we take more of a caseworker approach to helping people."

They proceeded and saw some of the shelter space, classrooms, dining facilities, and more.

"Hey, Mikey! Good to see you," Chris called out to a familiar face. A big smile and a wave ensued from the man he'd met on his first tour of TCC.

They concluded the tour by walking through the administrative area, meeting many of the program directors and the executive team, including David, the Chief Financial Officer. Everyone was friendly and casual, sharing an air of camaraderie with each other and with Michelle.

When they arrived back at the conference room, Michelle unlocked the door, and they filed in.

"Not only does that conclude our tour, but that also concludes our first training session," she said. "Remember, we'll be having another session soon, and the board retreat should be on your calendars. We're trying to pace the information so that you're not drinking from a fire hose. Thank you for your attentiveness, and I look forward to next time."

Chris knew everyone well enough to tell them goodbye by name as he left. He sat in the car for a few minutes, surprised at how exhausted he felt. It was that strange kind of exhaustion of being energized and yet wiped out at the same time. He couldn't wait to get home and tell Emily about the training, but he had already agreed to meet Michael for a run.

◆

As they ran along Barton Creek, Chris talked nonstop about the day's training session. "I learned so much about the people, the organization, and the homeless clients. We met a man named Scott. His story was amazing! Some people were even crying at the end. To be honest, I was a bit skeptical that any organization could make a meaningful difference here, but perhaps even small wins like Scott's are worth it."

Chris realized he had been talking for the better part of a mile, so he thought he should pass the baton. "What do you think, Michael? Do you think it's even possible to make a dent in the homeless issue in Austin?"

Michael was silent for a few strides, and they crossed a bridge busy with runners, walkers, and bikes. As Michael started to answer, he had to dodge a golden retriever barreling toward him. "Whoa, I think he likes me," Michael remarked, looking at the attractive woman on the other end of the leash. "He's a good judge of character," he quipped as everyone kept on running.

Michael looked back over his shoulder and smiled at the woman. She turned and smiled back. "Where were we?" he asked Chris.

"Before you got distracted, I asked if you thought we could make a difference in the homeless situation," Chris joked to his often flirtatious friend.

"I'm not sure. I think all of us in Austin hope that someone or some organization figures it out. It's ridiculous that people can just put up a tent anywhere and call it home. It certainly makes our city look trashy and unsafe. The problem is so big, though! Just look around us right here along this running trail... see how many makeshift homeless camps are set up?"

Chris noticed two tents, several shopping carts, some trash, and clothing hanging in the trees just before the bridge. He sighed and let his mind wander as Michael continued to talk about the vastness of the homeless issues in Austin. Maybe the problem was too big. Maybe all the time and effort poured into TCC was too little, too late.

The two friends ran silently the rest of the way back to the parking lot. Chris was frustrated. He'd gone from such an extreme high of excitement during the board training to feeling as if nothing could help.

During his final sprint to the end, Chris had an idea. Maybe he needed to understand the issue from the inside to see if there is any hope. He didn't want to spend the next three years serving on a board and volunteering for a hopeless cause. "I have enough demands on my time," he told himself. "I don't need to fill it with busy work that doesn't add any value. Plus, that's not what Jennifer intended when she announced all this. She wants us to find something worthwhile."

"I know!" Chris exclaimed suddenly. "Why don't I just invite a homeless person to lunch and find out what they think about the city's efforts to help them?"

Michael stared at Chris in disbelief. "Really? I get needing to know more, but I'm not sure that's how you want to gather your data. If you decide to do it, then I look forward to hearing how *that* goes," he snickered.

Perhaps Michael was right. But Chris knew that if he walked away from the idea that just popped into his head, he would never take the leap and try it. As Michael got in his car to leave, Chris lingered behind, stretching his hamstrings. As soon as the new BMW M3 exited the parking lot, Chris started jogging back to the tents he'd noticed earlier in the run.

◆ ◆ ◆

PERSONAL REFLECTION QUESTIONS FOR BOARD MEMBERS

Ask yourself the following questions and journal key points:

» What previous onboarding experiences for your work/ board were positive experiences for you? What made them positive?

» What onboarding experiences were negative? What made them negative?

» What do you feel are the most critical topics to cover during board onboarding?

» Which members of your board do you know the most, and which do you know the least?

GROUP DISCUSSION QUESTIONS FOR BOARD MEMBERS

With a group of other board members, discuss the following questions and note key points:

» Why do you think Chris is struggling so much with his decision to join the board?

» What improvements could/should be made to our board onboarding process?

» What role should our existing board members take regarding onboarding new members?

» Like Chris, how could we take an additional, hands-on step by going "back to the tents"? How might that help us be better board members?

SUGGESTED ACTIONS FOR BOARD MEMBERS

» **Bronze:** Take the time to visit with one staff member to learn more about them and their work.

» **Silver:** Take the executive director out for a meal and visit about the history of the organization, the needs related to your mission, and how they see your organization addressing them.

» **Gold:** Review your strategic plan, and look for ways to leverage your skills and relationships to make the greatest impact.

FOUR

Making Board Connections

CHRIS PULLED THE CHICKEN kabobs off the grill just as Emily and Jayden joined him on the back porch with a big salad and plates. "I cannot believe that we are grilling and eating outside in January," Emily chuckled.

"Let's enjoy it while we can!" Chris responded. Having grown up in California, Chris was accustomed to beautiful fair weather. He was surprised at how much the different extremes in Texas bothered him. "You know, when I moved to Texas, I had no idea what I was getting into weather-wise. It's southern, so I assumed the weather would be like California. Instead, it seems to be either hot or cold here, and the humidity makes the heat seem hotter and the cold even more miserable."

"Oh well," Emily chimed in. "On the rare days like today when the weather is near perfect, in January no less, we can be thankful and enjoy a nice dinner on the patio. A late dinner at that. You must have had a long run. What kept you so long?"

"Can I wait to answer?" Chris asked.

"Sure, do you have something else on your mind?"

"I would love to tell you and Jayden about my onboarding to the TCC board that I went to today," Chris said as he tried to gauge their level of interest. It was late, and Jayden must have been hungry since he was happily trying to cut a mushroom with a butter knife. Emily looked eager to hear more, so Chris shared some of the most memorable parts of the day.

"Something that was so interesting to me, which I hadn't even considered, was the new board members' diversity. I don't just mean race and gender. I mean their backgrounds, interests, experiences, and skills. I hadn't thought about who the other three new board members would be, but they ended up being the most interesting thing about the afternoon."

"Do you feel you will get along and be able to work well with them?" Emily questioned. She couldn't quite tell if Chris's use of the word "interesting" was a good thing or bad.

"I think so. I mean, it's a bit hard to tell at this point. They all bring something positive to the group. Susan, for example, has served on so many boards. Maybe more than a dozen. And she does a lot of volunteer work. She's the big question mark for me. I couldn't read her personality, but her experience alone will be valuable. LaShonda is so smart and engaging, plus she has a very personal passion for the homeless." Chris told Emily about LaShonda's brother. "Can you imagine?"

"No, I can't," Emily said, shaking her head slowly. "I'm kind of surprised that she wants to be involved with a cause that's likely so painful. But I can see the benefits of having someone with her passion. What about the fourth new member? What's their strength?"

"I'm going to like working with Juan, even if he is a bit

shy, or quiet—maybe both." Chris explained Juan's new role in his family business. "You know, TCC uses something called a board matrix of personal details to choose the members they need to recruit. I would think that TCC probably deals with some housing and facilities issues, and maybe Juan will be a good resource there."

"That sounds reasonable," Emily said. "So, why do you think Jennifer chose you?"

"She said my communication and presentation skills would be valuable, especially when presenting to other organizations that may donate to or partner with TCC. But she may be regretting that after today..."

Emily laughed. "Why is that?"

"Well, let me just say that I was less than eloquent in pretty much everything that came out of my mouth! At work I'm comfortable, and I know what I'm talking about. I have no problem sharing my thoughts and ideas. Today I was a bumbling mess, Em. Especially when I was introducing myself to the other new members. I'm sure they are all wondering why in the world I was asked to be on the board!"

Emily smiled empathetically. "Go easy on yourself. They were probably so focused on their own introductions that they didn't even notice your feeling like a fish out of water."

Jayden looked up from his food and cried, "Let's go fishing!" They all laughed together and nodded.

Chris breathed a sigh of relief. Emily had such a calming nature and always seemed to have the right thing to say when he needed encouragement. She was right. The other board members probably never knew how uncomfortable he was.

While they cleared the table after dinner, Chris explained he had another onboarding session the next Friday, followed by the first official board meeting at the end of the month.

Jayden fell asleep on the patio swing before 9:00. Chris scooped up his son to put him in bed. A bath and brushing Jayden's teeth would have to wait until tomorrow, along with the conversation about why his run took so long. Maybe he wouldn't mention that topic to Emily at all. He wasn't sure he was ready to talk about his encounter with a group of homeless people at Barton Creek quite yet.

◆

After a weekend of glorious weather, a few great runs, and a family trip to the Thinkery children's museum, Chris felt prepared to tackle another week in the office. His first meeting was with a group at 8:15 Monday morning. Just as he clicked "join" on the Zoom meeting link, Jennifer came into his office.

"Good morning! How was your weekend?" she asked in a chipper voice, a coffee cup in her hand as always.

Chris quickly muted his video conference. "It was great!" he said, pointing to his headset earpiece, letting her know he was on a call.

"Sorry about that! Hey, if you are having lunch in the breakroom, let's try to eat at the same time so we can chat about something," Jennifer whispered, forgetting he was on mute. Chris nodded affirmatively and re-focused his attention on his call.

"Hmm. I wonder what she wants to chat about now," he thought but quickly pushed the thought away when someone on the screen said his name.

◆

Around noon, Chris took his leftover kabobs out of the refrigerator in the break room and put them in the microwave. He walked to Jennifer's office to see if she was ready for lunch and met her just as she was exiting.

"Perfect timing!" she said.

They spent a few minutes preparing their lunches and sat at a table away from the hustle and bustle of the refrigerator and microwave. After some quick discussion about the extraordinarily wonderful weather and their weekends, Jennifer moved to the topic that was obviously on her mind.

"I hope the training on Friday was helpful. Did Michelle share with you the focus of the next session?" Jennifer asked.

"No, not specifically. She said the format would be different but no details."

"Okay, I hope I'm not spoiling your experience too much, but I want to tell you a little about what to expect. Last year, Michelle started something innovative—a mentoring program for new board members. She'd learned about the benefits of mentorship at a nonprofit leadership conference and decided to implement it. It worked out well, for the most part." Jennifer explained that Michelle had asked last year's new board members for feedback on the mentoring program. One thing they requested was more scheduled interaction with their mentors earlier in the year. "Basically," Jennifer continued, "some mentors did a great job of connecting, and others barely connected at all. Scheduling the connection time early on would allow the relationships more time to form and hopefully continue all year."

"Alright," Chris said. "You must have a reason for sharing this with me today, instead of waiting for Friday."

"Yes, Yoda. You are very perceptive," Jennifer said with a smile. "Michelle and I decided that I would be one of the mentors this year, so I will attend the program on Friday. I just wanted to let you know in advance that I am not going to be your mentor. I didn't want you to show up and assume I would be your mentor since I recruited you and because we already have a working relationship. That's all."

Chris thought for a moment. It would certainly be more comfortable and less awkward if Jennifer was his mentor. They wouldn't have to go through the "getting to know each other" phase, but it was probably best for both of them to connect with new people.

"Okay, that makes sense," Chris responded thoughtfully.

"Really? You aren't upset?" Jennifer seemed surprised.

"No, I mean, you are already like a mentor to me here at work. I think pairing up with someone different at TCC makes sense. Any idea who it will be?"

"Well, everyone will find out on Friday, so I better not spoil things any more than I have. Honestly, the person Michelle selected for you is one of the board members I don't know well, so I wouldn't have much to share anyway."

"Who are you going to mentor?" Chris was curious to know.

"Susan. She has a lot of board experience that I think will be great for our board, and I can learn a lot from her. She also seems eager to move into a board leadership position, so I'll help groom her for that."

Chris was curious why Susan was interested in a leadership position on the board when she'd seemed distracted at best and disinterested at worst the other day. Maybe Chris read her wrong, or maybe she was having an off day. He knew he'd had his share of those. Either way, Jennifer was such a great leader, and if anyone could mentor a future leader, it was her.

Jennifer was thankful that Chris was very accepting, even supportive, of her not mentoring him. She had been concerned throughout the weekend about how he would respond to that decision.

Jennifer and Chris enjoyed the rest of their lunch break, mixing conversation about work projects and their families. They didn't eat together often, but they both enjoyed it when they did. As their time wrapped up, Chris had a thought.

"Hey, it's always great having lunch and catching up with each other. We need to do it more often. I know you aren't going to be my formal mentor at TCC, but like I said, you are still a mentor to me. Are you open to setting a more frequent lunch check-in? I'm thinking of no specific agenda; we can talk about anything. Would you be up for that?"

"I think that is a great idea!" Jennifer responded. "Let's set it up."

After putting their dishes in the dishwasher, they parted ways, and Chris sent an invite for their next scheduled lunch meeting.

◆

As the week went on, Chris became more anxious to learn who his mentor would be and what he might learn from him or her. Friday's onboarding session at TCC was scheduled to begin at 2:00. Chris asked Emily to join him for lunch at 12:30 so he could head to his meeting afterward.

They met at True Food Kitchen downtown, one of Emily's favorite lunch spots where the menu changed seasonally. Emily ordered butternut squash soup, and Chris ordered a roasted Brussels sprout bowl with hummus.

Emily quickly jumped in with a question, which Chris could tell she had been waiting to ask when the opportunity presented itself. "You never shared with me why you were so late from your run last Friday. Was everything alright with Michael?"

"Oh. Yep, Michael was fine. We had a great run. He mostly listened and kept the running pace fast as I went on and on about my training that afternoon. I was debating whether TCC actually made a difference when suddenly I had the thought that maybe I needed to talk to someone who is homeless to find out what they think."

"Good idea! Perhaps you could visit TCC next week and meet up with someone," Emily suggested.

"Well, actually, I already did meet up with somebody. Not at TCC, though. That's why I waited to talk to you about it. While we were running, I noticed a homeless camp near a bridge along the trail. I knew that if I didn't act right then, I would likely chicken out. So, when Michael left, I ran back to the camp and met three people living there—two men and a woman. I asked if I could bring them lunch one day, and they were eager to say yes. Yesterday, I picked up sandwiches and chips at Thundercloud Subs and walked back to their camp to deliver lunch. Not only were they surprised to see me, but they were also shocked when I asked to join them!"

"You had lunch out at their camp?" Emily asked incredulously.

"Yes! Pam looked to be around 45 and was the most talkative of the group. The others seemed a bit older, though it was hard to tell. Bill never said a word. I only knew his name because Pam told me. Glen wasn't as talkative as Pam, but still joined in the conversation some."

"What did you talk about?"

"Thankfully, Pam carried a lot of the conversation. She was hard to follow, jumping from topic to topic. I casually tried to ask questions to learn about any experiences they had with nonprofits. I wanted to know if they ever went to places like TCC for meals and other resources. Surprisingly, Pam said they'd heard that places like that were just trying to get something out of you."

"Like what?"

"For one thing, Pam said they only tried to get homeless people to change. According to her, all they talked about was learning the right skills to get a job and how so many of the homeless 'needed' counseling. But Pam says they love the carefree life they live. They didn't want to bother with someone else getting in their business."

"Wow! That isn't what I was expecting," Emily said. "What, if anything, did you tell them about why you were there?"

"I just said that I saw them while I was running and thought they would enjoy a sandwich. I only stayed about 30 minutes. I had quite a walk back to the car and needed to get to an afternoon meeting. I'm glad I went, though. Seeing where and how the homeless live was eye-opening. The fact that those three wanted to live that way was beyond what I could comprehend.

It got me thinking that the problem of homelessness is much deeper than I imagined."

"Did the experience make you want to be more or less involved at TCC?"

Chris thought a moment. "I'm not sure. It makes me worried even more that the issue is too big to fix. At the same time, Pam's insights kind of sparked some energy in me."

"How so?"

"I have a bit of inside scoop now. There are homeless people in Austin who don't use the services available because they see them as untrustworthy. Think about some of the situations these folks have come from...abuse, neglect, poverty. Of course, they don't trust others. Pam feels as if someone is always trying to 'get something' from her. We need to be aware that some of our clients believe this way. How can places like TCC help, if they can't even reach the ones who need the most help?"

"That's a good point," Emily said after a few moments of silence. "So, does that mean you are all in?"

"I hadn't thought of it that way, but I guess so. Pam put a face on the reason why TCC exists. But TCC may not even know people like her exist. I wonder if—or how—we can reach those who don't want to be reached."

Emily grinned and said, "I thought you must be all in when I heard you say the word 'we'!" She looked at her watch. "Yikes, you have to go! I'll get the bill, and you head out."

Chris hurried, knowing he had just enough time to make it to the training without being late.

◆

Chris walked in with only a minute to spare.

"I was about to text you. I wondered if maybe you got caught up at the office," Jennifer said.

"No, I was having lunch with Emily, and time slipped away."

"Welcome back everyone!" Michelle said, kicking off the meeting. "I'm glad we didn't scare anyone off last week and that you all returned for the second training session. Today will be a very different experience. As I'm sure you have noticed, Jennifer is joining us again, along with three other board members—meet Natalie, Roger, and Darius."

They had been on the board for at least two years and were all entering the final year of their first term, except Darius, who was halfway through his second term. All three, plus Jennifer, had volunteered to participate in TCC's new board member mentorship program.

Michelle continued explaining details about her vision for the mentorship program. First, Michelle wanted new members to feel welcome and connected upon arriving at their first board meeting. She hoped having a mentor would ease any anxiety and make new members more comfortable so that they would participate and collaborate from the beginning.

"Each of you will be partnered with a mentor and receive a $10 gift card to a coffee shop nearby. Your mentor also has some conversation starters that will get the discussion going. We will meet back here at 3:30 to debrief your time together and answer any questions. And we should end promptly at 4:00, so you can get your weekend started."

Michelle asked each mentor to stand up and announce who their mentee for the year would be. Jennifer announced that she would mentor Susan. Natalie went next and paired up with LaShonda. Roger would partner with Chris. That left Darius, who joked that Juan was stuck with him by default. Everyone chuckled and stood awkwardly, not knowing what to do next. Thankfully, Michelle jumped in with her usual enthusiasm. "Okay, grab a gift card and head out. See you back at 3:30."

Roger got a gift card and met Chris at the door. "Nice to meet you, Chris," he said, extending a hand.

"Hi. Thanks for agreeing to mentor me this year," Chris said, returning the handshake.

It was only a two-minute walk to the quaint but bustling corner coffee shop just one street over.

◆

Roger went to order drinks, and Chris found a table for them. Apparently, 2:30 on a Friday was a popular time to get coffee. Many tables were already taken, and four people were in line before Roger. However, the baristas were efficient, and within five minutes, Roger joined Chris with a chai tea and a soy latte in hand.

"So, tell me a little about yourself, Chris," Roger said to kick off their conversation.

"Well, I'm not sure where to start. Let's see. I work for Sharp Edge Marketing, the same firm that Jennifer works for. I love my job, the people, and the environment. I'm a senior account executive, so basically, I listen to the needs and desires of the client and then work with a team to make it happen. When I'm not working, I try to run often. My wife, Emily, and I have one son, Jayden, so that also keeps me busy. How about you?"

"I also have a family," Roger began, "which seems to be making me more and more busy as the years pass. I have two in high school right now, and most evenings are filled with practices and events. I'm not married to their mom anymore, and the kids mostly live with her. So I try to attend everything I can, even practices, if I'm able to squeeze it in."

Chris was thankful to find something in common with Roger. They spent some time swapping stories about kids' sporting events, crazy parents, bad calls, biased coaches, and why they love watching despite the inevitable drama. When one of the sports stories seemed to trail off, Chris asked, "What type of work do you do?"

"I'm in commercial real estate. I used to do residential, but I ran into a college buddy of mine four years ago, and a few beers later, I agreed to join his commercial firm. It's been more of an adjustment than I thought it would be, but I'm enjoying learning something new."

Roger then pivoted to the questions Michelle had given each mentor. "Okay, let's see. What led you to join the TCC board?" he asked Chris, reading from a sheet of paper.

"I would love to say that I have always dreamed of giving back to my community this way. But to be honest, I hadn't ever even considered it! At work, the senior leaders asked all the managers to get involved with a nonprofit organization in a meaningful way. And my search to meet that requirement led me here. But I'm getting pretty excited the more I learn about TCC. What about you? What led you to join the TCC board,

Roger?"

Chris wasn't expecting the answer he received.

"It wasn't my idea. As I said, I joined my buddy's real estate firm. He got me to apply for a community leadership program called Leadership Austin where he serves on their board," Roger began. "He said that it would be a great way for me to network with others, but as it turned out, the program just focuses on meeting our community's needs. My peers were all gung-ho to join boards and volunteer at the end. I felt peer pressure to follow suit. We'd toured TCC on one of our Leadership Austin field trips, and it was close to my office and home, so I chose it!"

Chris nodded. "It sounds as if both of us ended up here through some pressure. Now that you're involved at TCC, what are your thoughts?" He hoped Roger was going to tell how he'd since become inspired about serving at TCC. No such luck.

"It's fine," Roger said nonchalantly. "I mean, I attend the meetings, and I find them mildly interesting. The people seem nice. I didn't have any expectations and didn't have anything to compare with my experience. I don't think I'm a model board member, if I'm shooting straight with you."

Roger's indifference caught Chris off guard. It seemed odd. Why would Roger volunteer to be a mentor if he wasn't very enthused about TCC and didn't even desire to be more engaged?

"What made you decide to become a mentor?" Chris probed.

"During a meeting near the end of last year, Michelle shared with us various opportunities to be more involved this year. It sounded like an expectation that we join a committee or project. There was a fundraising committee, a committee that planned the yearly gala, a group to recruit new board members, and so on. None of them sounded like anything I had the time to do. I decided mentoring was the best choice for me. I get along with people, and I enjoy free coffee," he said with a sarcastic smile as he raised his cup.

Chris laughed hesitantly, hoping Roger would ask another one of Michelle's questions so they could move the conversation along. Thankfully, another question wasn't necessary. Chris noticed LaShonda and Natalie standing up and gathering their coats, so he checked his watch. It was 3:19. "I guess we better start back to TCC," he said.

"Yep, it's about that time," Roger agreed, and the two men left.

◆

Back in the TCC conference room, the chatter was considerably louder than it had been earlier. Apparently, the "getting to know you" coffee time was a success for the other pairings. The laughter and conversation were so boisterous that Michelle had to raise her volume to draw the group in for the debrief session.

"How was it?" she began.

"It was a great way to spend the afternoon," LaShonda said.

"I completely agree," Darius added.

"What did you like about it?" Michelle questioned.

"Everything, really," Darius answered. "The coffee was great, and the company was even better. Juan is a neat guy, and it was a privilege to get to know him. Kudos to whoever...or is it whomever...recommended him. He is going to be a huge asset to the board."

Juan looked a little embarrassed by the attention but smiled genuinely. "I am glad we had the opportunity to do this. It was time well spent."

Chris looked around the room and noticed everyone was nodding their agreement. He felt a little guilty that he didn't feel the same. Roger seemed like a nice enough guy, but he didn't find much value in their conversation. Maybe they just didn't have enough time. Perhaps he could invite Roger to lunch next week and get to know him better.

By the time Chris stopped his internal dialogue and joined back in the discussion, everyone was wrapping up and getting ready to leave. Chris started looking around to gather his stuff as others stood up to say their good-byes.

"Hey Roger, thanks again for today. I want to continue our conversation if you're up for it. How about lunch next week?"

"Oh, yeah, let me see how my week looks. What's your number, and I'll let you know?"

They exchanged numbers, shook hands, and Roger headed toward the door. Chris saw Jennifer crossing the room toward him. "How was your coffee meeting?" she asked.

"It was fine. Roger seems like a nice guy. How was yours?"

"Fine," she said. Jennifer picked up on Chris's hesitation. He seemed to be holding back, but she wasn't sure why. Then again, she hadn't been candid with him either about her uneasy meeting with Susan.

"Susan also seems nice. I mean, as far as I could tell," she added.

"Hmmm," Chris thought. "That doesn't sound convincing. I wonder what happened."

They both stood silently for a moment, soaking in the

uneasy feelings they both shared.

"Well, maybe we can debrief at our next lunch check-in," Chris said finally.

"Sure, I think that is a great idea. I would like to hear more about how it went with Roger and get some input on my mentorship with Susan."

Jennifer had a sickening feeling as Chris walked out of the conference room. She had been so excited to bring Chris on and start a new year with TCC. Now, she was beginning to question all of it. "What if we made some wrong decisions about choosing these board members? What if we are going in the wrong direction altogether?" she wondered.

Jennifer gathered her notebook and phone and then dug through her purse to find her keys. The enthusiasm she'd felt just hours ago had faded, replaced with uncertainty and dread.

❖ ❖ ❖

PERSONAL REFLECTION QUESTIONS FOR BOARD MEMBERS
Ask yourself the following questions and journal key points:

» What aspect of being a board member could you improve upon? Who could mentor you on that aspect?

» What questions can you ask of fellow board members to help you know them better?

» How does knowing your fellow board members benefit the organization and you?

» What parts of your organization would you like to know more about?

Group Discussion Questions for Board Members

With a group of other board members, discuss the following questions and note key points:

» How are we similar, and how are we different?

» How do our differences make us better equipped as a board?

» How can we learn to depend upon one another's strengths and trust one another more?

Suggested Actions for Board Members

» **Bronze:** Actively communicate with your mentor, if you are assigned one. If your board doesn't have a mentor program, reach out to a fellow board member to meet.

» **Silver:** Before your next board meeting, invite three other board members to get together (assuming that doesn't make up a quorum), strictly to get to know each other better.

» **Gold:** Help create or improve your existing board mentorship program.

FIVE

One Awkward Board Meeting

EMILY AND CHRIS SET up lawn chairs in the driveway to watch Jayden and his neighborhood friends ride their scooters and bikes before sunset. They sat quietly for a few minutes, enjoying hearing Jayden's laugh and seeing him smile.

"Oh, I've meant to ask you how your second training went at TCC," Emily said as Jayden zoomed past them with six-year-old Katelyn from next door chasing right behind him.

"Well, it was fine. It wasn't like the first one was. We each partnered up with a mentor from the board and went down the street for a get-to-know-you coffee meeting."

"That sounds like a great way to find out more about the other board members and learn about the position."

"Yes, you would think that…" Chris said. Emily clearly saw that his body language communicated more than his few words.

She followed up. "Did it not go well?"

"I'm not sure. My mentor, Roger, seemed nice, but I just didn't get the vibe from him that I expected to."

Emily wondered why Chris seemed unsure about his mentor. She debated asking more questions but got the sense that Chris didn't want to say much. Emily decided to let the conversation go for now but would mention to Chris later that perhaps he should meet with Jennifer and share his thoughts with her.

After tucking Jayden into bed and reading bedtime stories, Emily brought up the subject carefully. "I got the sense earlier that you have some things on your mind about the TCC session, or your mentor, or both. When is your next lunch to touch base with Jennifer? Maybe she would be a good sounding board."

"That's a good idea. I know she's busy, but she may have some time."

Emily made a guiding suggestion in the form of a question. "Could you text her and ask?"

Chris took his phone and texted Jennifer.

Hey, time this week for lunch?

Ding. The quick response surprised him.

Yep. Wednesday?

Chris responded with a thumbs up.

"Okay, it's set with Jennifer. Lunch on Wednesday."

Emily felt relieved. "That's great. How about I make your favorite grilled chicken and feta pitas for your lunch Wednesday, and you can take enough for both of you?"

"That would be great. I'm sure Jennifer will love the pitas. I'll let her know lunch is on you." Once again, Chris was thankful to be married to a foodie. She not only had a way with words; she had a way with food.

◆

By the time Wednesday's lunch with Jennifer rolled around, Chris had processed his time with Roger. His first impression was that Roger was disengaged. He didn't seem to have any interest in TCC and didn't say much to help Chris's onboarding. Why would Michelle choose Roger to be his mentor? He hoped maybe Jennifer would have some insight.

Jennifer had also been thinking about her meeting with Susan over the weekend. Michelle had said so many wonderful things about Susan. Up until their meeting, Jennifer even anticipated Susan being board chair someday. Jennifer got a strange gut feeling about Susan now, and she wondered if perhaps Susan had some other motive for joining the board.

She couldn't quite put her finger on the apprehensive feeling. Susan just seemed to come to the mentoring meeting with an agenda other than getting to know each other and learning about TCC. Of course, Jennifer also recognized that sometimes it was challenging for her to connect with people who had very different personalities from her own.

"Just because I didn't seem to connect with Susan doesn't mean she won't be a valuable board member. In fact, diverse views, perspectives, and personalities are needed on a board," Jennifer told herself convincingly. At the same time, Jennifer knew well that dissension on the board would be detrimental, so she decided to keep an eye on Susan's motives and give her the benefit of the doubt for now. She would see how things played out.

Jennifer and Chris sat down to enjoy their chicken pita

lunch, and Chris jumped right in with questions. "So, what do you know about Roger?"

"Not much," Jennifer replied. "He has always seemed easygoing and a bit quiet. Michelle said he's shy and that being a mentor will be a good experience for him. Why?"

"He didn't seem shy to me. I'm not sure how to explain it. Maybe he was just having an off day. I just expected to hear more from him since he's been on the board for two years."

"My meeting with Susan was also a surprise. She asked a lot of questions, but not the ones I anticipated."

"Like what?" Chris was curious to know.

"She asked me a lot about Michelle. 'Is she doing a good job? What do you like and not like about her leadership? Do you see her staying at TCC?' I don't know why she was so interested in Michelle, but that is all she wanted to talk about..." She thought, but chose not to say, that Susan was like a dog on a bone.

Chris agreed that it was strange for Susan to ask so many questions about Michelle.

The two spent the rest of their lunch talking about how odd their mentor/mentee meetings went. Their conversation didn't seem to make any progress other than allowing them to vent and think out loud about the situations.

Just before they parted, Chris remembered to ask Jennifer how to prepare for the first official upcoming board meeting.

"You know, that's what a board mentor is for," Jennifer pointed out. "This is an opportunity for us to connect with Roger and Susan. Even though both of our meetings didn't go as we had expected, I think it is important for us to keep an open mind. I'll call Susan and talk to her about the first meeting, and you call Roger and ask for his input on how to prepare for it. This will give us a good reason to reach out and hopefully connect better this time around."

Chris was once again impressed at how quick-witted Jennifer was. She seemed to pull great ideas out of thin air. He always learned so much from her and wished she could be his mentor at TCC instead of Roger. But Jennifer was right. He should give Roger another try, so he picked up his phone and called him.

◆

Soon it was time for the first board meeting of the year. Chris was excited to attend. He had talked to Roger and felt good about their phone conversation. Roger sounded surprised by the call but was more friendly and open.

As was his custom, Chris arrived at the TCC conference room at 3:55, five minutes before the meeting was set to begin. Not too early and not late.

"Hi Chris!" welcomed Michelle. "So glad to see you! Your name card is right over there," she said, pointing across the table. Chris noticed the empty seat next to his had Roger's tent name card on it. He sat down and said his hellos to the others around him.

At precisely 4:00 Jennifer announced they had a quorum, and the meeting was called to order. Chris had heard the word "quorum" but wasn't quite sure exactly what that meant in this context, so he took a note to ask someone later.

Then he wondered, "Or should I ask questions along the way? I wonder what the protocol is?" He didn't know.

Just then, Roger walked in and said, "Sorry for being late.

My afternoon meeting ran long."

Chris decided to ask Roger his questions after the meeting.

"Okay, hopefully everyone had an opportunity to review the consent agenda and financial statements prior to the meeting," Jennifer was saying when Chris focused back in. He had no idea what Jennifer was talking about. He looked around the room and noticed all the other board members leafing through documents they had brought to the meeting. He scanned near the door to see if maybe he missed the handouts on the way in. Nothing.

"Where did everyone get those?" he whispered to Roger.

"They were sent by email a few days ago," Roger whispered back.

Chris's mind raced, and he felt conspicuously awkward without the documents needed for the meeting. Did he miss the email? Did the email go to his spam folder? Did Michelle accidentally leave him off the distribution list? Chris prided himself in being on top of things, and this meeting wasn't starting out positively. He picked up his pen and noted two additional questions to ask Roger after the meeting:

1. What is a consent agenda?
2. Why didn't you tell me I needed to find and print documents before the meeting?

Chris pulled his focus to Jennifer and tried to concentrate on what she was saying. He straightened his pocket square, realizing that's what he tended to do when he felt uncomfortable.

"I want to give a shout-out to one of our new board members, LaShonda," Jennifer said. "Even though this is her first board meeting, she has already been very active as an ambassador for TCC. You may have noticed that she commented on and shared each of our social media posts, helping spread the word about TCC. It's that kind of exposure that we hope you all feel compelled to provide."

"Social media?" Chris thought. He didn't even use social media, other than taking an occasional glance at LinkedIn. "Am I supposed to be doing something on social media? Ugh." Chris took another note about the board's expectation for social media. His list of questions was growing longer by the minute!

Once again, Jennifer's voice jolted him from his own habitual internal ramblings. As he re-engaged, he heard Susan correcting Jennifer, but he wasn't quite sure what she was correcting. Something about not needing a motion for something.

Jennifer's face turned a pale shade of red, but her voice remained calm and collected. "Okay. Thanks, Susan," Jennifer said.

The group moved on to the next order of business. The room was uncomfortably quiet as Jennifer continued. Chris added to his notes: What was the issue with the motion?

Jennifer then called on Michelle to give the executive director's report. At the end of the report, one of the board members said, "I make a motion to accept the executive director's report."

Susan immediately stated, "That isn't needed. The chair can just move to the next order of business."

Jennifer and Michelle looked at each other, unsure how to move forward. Was Susan trying to prove a point? Did she want to look good or knowledgeable in front of the board?

"What is happening?" Chris wondered. "Why is Susan

bringing up all of these issues with how Jennifer is running the meeting?"

Jennifer moved on to the next topic on the agenda. "Okay, Leah has a committee report for our fall event called Beyond the Bridge. And for you new members who don't know, Leah is serving a second term on the board and was the recipient of the Ambassador Award last year."

Chris felt totally lost. He wrote in his notes: "What is the Ambassador Award?"

Before he had even finished writing, Michelle spoke up. "Jennifer, let me add something please about the award. Every year, our mayor gives the Ambassador Award to a volunteer in our community. We liked that idea, so we do our own version of the award each year to highlight what we want to see our volunteers do."

Leah then shared how the upcoming Beyond the Bridge activity would feature many events throughout the community to build awareness and serve the homeless in various ways. TCC still needed a few people to join the Beyond the Bridge committee, including someone who could deliver a presentation to the Rotary Club in two weeks. Leah wouldn't be able to attend and needed someone to present in her place.

Chris tentatively raised his hand. "I can be on the committee. I don't feel ready to present now, but if you help equip me, I can do the Rotary meeting also."

"Wonderful, Chris! Thank you!" Leah beamed, which made Chris smile broadly. He wasn't exactly sure what all he had just committed to, but he felt good about finding a way to contribute.

The rest of the meeting was a blur. Jennifer and Michelle

grew more frazzled as Susan continued to challenge the way Jennifer ran the meeting.

At the end of the day, Michelle reminded them to look for an email soon about the board member retreat, stating that it would be for a half-day in the Austin area. But everyone seemed distracted and uncomfortable by now, and people left quickly when the meeting adjourned. Chris had hoped to talk with Roger a few minutes and ask him the questions he wrote down, but Roger headed for the door without even saying goodbye. The mood of the room was not one where chatter seemed appropriate. Jennifer and Michelle had also exited quickly to talk privately in Michelle's office. Chris gathered up his belongings and walked to his car. His first board meeting did not go at all like he expected.

◆

After the meeting, Chris met up with Michael for a run. There was a chill in the air, so Chris was hoping for a fast pace to keep him warm. He also thought this may be a good time to talk about the odd way Susan behaved at the meeting.

"So, I just went to my first board meeting today, and one of the new board members named Susan kept interjecting negative feedback on how the meeting was run...like motions...and what could and could not be tabled. I'm not even sure how Susan knows how the meeting should or should not go. Doesn't the board chair decide that?"

"Oh, well, it sounds like she is a stickler for *Robert's Rules*."

"Robert's Rules? Who's Robert?" Chris asked sincerely.

Michael chuckled, "I have no idea, but *Robert's Rules* is a manual that outlines how meetings that follow parliamentary procedure should be conducted. I don't know much, but it has a lot of nit-picky rules about who can say what and when they can say it. It's meant to keep order, and it does that, but it's a little too formal for my taste. If you want to know more, then I'm sure you can look online and learn plenty without actually reading the book."

Before bed Chris searched for *Robert's Rules*. Michael was right. He quickly found more information than he ever wanted.

Chris discovered that *Robert's Rules of Order* is the standard manual used during parliamentary meetings, such as board meetings. The book was first published in 1876 by Henry Martyn Robert, a U.S. Army Colonel, to provide a detailed way to handle every aspect of running a meeting, such as discussions and voting. The first publication of the book included 176 pages and was meant to be a brief and simple guide for leaders of meetings. Just five months later, Captain Robert released a second edition that included more specific situations not addressed in the first edition. In 2011 the eleventh edition was published and included a whopping 698 pages of rules, including references to technological advancement considerations. While the first edition was intended to be user-friendly, the rules within the most recent edition looked painstakingly complex to Chris. But its widespread popularity and acceptance led many nonprofit organizations to adopt the *Rules* as part of their bylaws and procedures.

"Hmmm, well, Susan has been on a lot of boards, so I guess that's why she knows so much about *Robert's Rules*," Chris said out loud without realizing it.

"Who is Robert?" Emily asked, walking up behind him and

planting a kiss on his cheek.

"Ha! I had a similar question earlier today," Chris said. He told Emily what he'd learned. He could see why many nonprofits found the *Rules* helpful in maintaining order and fairness during meetings, but he could also clearly see challenges already.

Understanding how to implement 698 pages of rules was not an easy task and not one that Chris imagined most board members were equipped to take on. Having a board member like Susan regularly interjecting, "That's not what *Robert's Rules* says..." might be helpful in some situations, but it could also cause problems.

"It was exhausting and frustrating," Chris said as he told his wife about Susan's bewildering actions. "But I do have some good news. I volunteered to be on the Beyond the Bridge committee."

"I've heard Michelle talk about that event! That sounds great. What will your role be?"

"I'm not exactly sure, but I think my first task will be to present to the Rotary Club. They helped with Beyond the Bridge last year, and we hope they will help again this year. I guess it depends on how convincing I am," Chris joked.

"I'm sure you will be charming as usual and they won't be able to say no," Emily teased in return. "Hey, maybe Jayden and I can also help in some way."

"I would love that," Chris said softly. Little did he know then that none of them would make it to Beyond the Bridge.

◆ ◆ ◆

PERSONAL REFLECTION QUESTIONS FOR BOARD MEMBERS

Ask yourself the following questions and journal key points:

» How prepared are you usually for board meetings?

» How can you be supportive of healthy and productive board meetings?

» What seems to be missing in your board meetings?

GROUP DISCUSSION QUESTIONS FOR BOARD MEMBERS

With a group of other board members, discuss the following questions and note key points:

» Are we clear regarding our agreed-upon procedures for board meetings? Are the procedures stated or unstated?

» Do we tap into the expertise that is in the room at board meetings? Explain.

» What could we do in our board meetings to make the organization even stronger?

» What could be done in our board meetings to further equip our board members?

SUGGESTED ACTIONS FOR BOARD MEMBERS

» **Bronze:** Be certain you understand the meeting procedures of your board.

» **Silver:** Commit to being prepared for every board meeting.

» **Gold:** Encourage and challenge other board members to be equipped and prepared for board meetings.

SIX

Finding the Fit

EVER SINCE THE FIRST board meeting, Chris had been anxious to meet with Jennifer and get her take on all the drama. He was still a bit upset with Roger for not telling him how to prepare for the meeting, and then there was Susan.

Chris heated up his zucchini stir-fry leftovers from the amazing meal Emily made the night before. As always, Emily made sure to send plenty for Jennifer as well.

"Hey, Chris! Something smells great!" Jennifer said as she set her lunch bag down on a table and walked to the sink to wash her hands.

"Well, Emily sent some for you, too."

"That's just another reason I love our lunch meetings. Perhaps we should do them more often," Jennifer joked. It had been almost a month since they had been able to catch up about Travis County Cares.

"We have a lot going on internally and externally at TCC. By the way, thanks for stepping up to be on the committee!

Your sales and marketing expertise is going to be super helpful to us."

"I hope I didn't bite off more than I can chew," Chris said humbly. "It's a good way to leverage our skills and abilities here at Sharp Edge. I'm also speaking to the Downtown Rotary tomorrow."

Right then, Preston ran in with a smile on his face and an iPad in his hand. "I'm so glad I caught you two," he said. "I need you to sign up for your spot in next week's blood drive. I'll have the mobile unit out front."

Jennifer's face went flush as Chris started to sign up. "Do you have plenty of spots for everyone?" she asked, secretly hoping that he didn't have any availability.

"We're getting great traction, but I can add a second day if I need to. In fact, Lisa in accounting suggested reaching out to others in the building, and that proved to be successful."

Jennifer thought about trying to come up with an excuse, but instead, she planted a smile on her face and took the device from Chris to sign up.

As she finished writing her name in a time slot, she cheerfully said to Preston, "You're making a big difference, Preston! Well done!"

"Thanks for signing up, y'all," he said as he roared off to recruit the next unsuspecting volunteers.

After he was out of earshot, Jennifer looked at Chris and said, "He's become an excellent vampire! I'm proud of him, but truth be told, I hate giving blood."

"Leadership has its costs!" Chris bantered.

Jennifer rolled her eyes. "So, where were we?"

"I'll jump right in. Was that a typical board meeting? I felt like I was on a *Jerry Springer Show* episode."

Jennifer nearly spewed the Coconut La Croix she was drinking. "No! That was not typical. I feel terrible about your first board meeting. I talked to Michelle afterward, and she was as shocked as I was by Susan's behavior."

"That is comforting, I guess. It wasn't just me who thought it didn't go well."

"No, you aren't the only one. I was surprised by Susan's dominant stance on *Robert's Rules*. Given her experience, I assumed she would know a lot about how board meetings should run, but I didn't expect her to be so vocal! I'm torn on what to think. I understand the rules of order and don't intentionally want to mess them up. But at the same time, the constant disruptions about how we weren't following the rules was so distracting."

"I agree!" Chris piped in. "And for someone like me who knows nothing at all about *Robert's Rules*, I'm not very encouraged to take a leadership role. We are volunteers and don't need to be called out continuously while we're trying to do the best we can. I felt so bad for you!"

"Me too. I was embarrassed for myself and for Susan. I'm having coffee with her next week as her mentor, and this will certainly be part of the discussion. First, I want her to help me with understanding the basic rules better. But I also need to make sure she understands that she cannot continue interrupting. It upsets the flow and mood of the meeting."

Jennifer changed directions. "Speaking of mentoring, how are things going with Roger?"

"We don't have any plans to meet, but I'm okay with that for now. You know, I called Roger before the board meeting to ask him how to prepare. He said there was nothing I needed to do, and then I see everyone else had printed and reviewed documents in advance! I was pretty irritated."

"Didn't you get the email from Michelle?"

"No, it went to my spam folder, so I didn't see it. If Roger had said something to remind me, then I would have looked for it before the meeting. I thought that's what a board mentor was for."

"Oh, that stinks. I'm not sure why Roger didn't tell you. Don't worry, with the way Susan was acting, I don't think anyone even noticed that you didn't have the documents and hadn't prepared."

This was probably true, but Chris wondered what else Roger wasn't telling him. "So, what all does TCC expect of its board members anyway?"

"Hmmmm," Jennifer tapped her fork as she thought. "That's a good question. You know, I need some more time to gather my thoughts to answer that completely. It may be a good topic for a board meeting. Or, we may even bring it up at the board retreat. That will be a perfect item to cover. Thanks for the great idea!"

"No problem, that's what I'm here for," Chris said.

Jennifer moved on to the next topic. "How do you see Sharp Edge getting involved in the big event?"

"Beyond the Bridge?" Chris asked.

Jennifer nodded with her mouth full.

Watching her eyes to gauge her reaction, Chris said, "In our first committee meeting, they talked about how poorly last year's communication efforts with the public went. They felt that the event could have made a significantly greater impact.

Michelle even called it 'Austin's best-kept secret!'"

Jennifer cut him off. "Which means we sucked at marketing it."

Chris nodded affirmatively and launched into summarizing his progress so far. He had already visited with the graphics, media, and social media departments. They were busy creating collateral material for a promotion plan. "With moderate effort at our office, we can make this a big deal," he said with more excitement than even he expected.

Jennifer was pleased. "Any roadblocks here?"

"Our marketing guys are pretty tied up right now. But I've got Beyond the Bridge on their calendar, and they assure me it'll be done by the deadline. I may be a little nervous about speaking tomorrow, but I'll get over it."

"I'm not concerned about you," Jennifer said with a mysterious look on her face. She had lots of concerns to occupy her thoughts. Her daughter, Sarah, was in her junior year of college and was suddenly struggling with grades. Business was good, but they weren't hitting the growth numbers they were aiming for. And that last board meeting felt like a disaster! The least of her worries was Chris's ability to speak in front of a group about TCC.

◆

Many months passed, and Chris worked hard as the main marketing and communication source related to Beyond the Bridge. On September 5th, one week before the event, the committee gathered for final planning and preparations. The room was full of energy and excitement as each member provided updates.

Juan spoke up first. "The materials are all purchased, and we have leaders for each crew of volunteers for the construction projects. My people will have everything laid out by 6:00 a.m. that day."

Chris smiled and gave him a thumbs up. Their friendship was growing, and he was impressed with Juan's ability to get things done. There were six significant construction-related projects planned, and Juan was spearheading all of them.

Natalie was next on the agenda and shared about volunteer check-in, t-shirts, and snacks.

David, the CFO of TCC, was next. He updated everyone on the budget, insurance, and transportation.

When it was Chris's turn, he straightened his bright green pocket square before he spoke. "We've had interviews on all the morning shows and have completed speaking engagements at 12 different clubs. I pulled the social media reports, and our ad had been seen by 28,549 people when I left the office. Lots of shares, likes, and comments. We've got some mojo!"

Juan looked at him quizzically and asked, "Mojo?"

"You know, energy. Momentum."

Juan smiled and elbowed Chris. "Okay, mow joe!"

While the reports about food distribution, volunteers, supplies, and more continued, Chris looked at his watch. "I've got to get out of here," he thought. "Emily will kick me if I'm late again, especially with our friends coming over for dinner tonight."

◆

That night, Michael joined Chris, Emily, Jayden, and Emily's friend Candice in the backyard. Chris had only met Candice a few times. She shared Emily's enthusiasm for eating healthy and working out, and she was a regular at the same spin class. Emily was testing some new recipes tonight and had invited Candice as a taste-tester.

Candice complimented the dinner. "Everything's great guys, thanks for having me over. The veggies are crazy fresh."

Emily smiled and bragged on the farmers at the farmer's market. "Why were you so late, Chris? Tough day at work?"

"No. Sorry about that. We had a committee meeting for Beyond the Bridge!"

Candice perked up. "That's the event that Michelle told us about at spin class," she said, looking at Emily. "She's with um, ah..."

"Travis County Cares," Chris said to help her out.

Candice continued, "Right! I'm signed up to register volunteers that morning."

"Well, then you'll see me there," Michael said. Emily and Chris nearly sprained their necks to look at Michael with shocked expressions.

"What? You don't think attorneys volunteer?" Michael asked loudly but with a grin on his face.

"It's just that..." Chris said, his voice trailing off as he tried to choose his words carefully.

"Maybe you're just rubbing off on me a little," Michael interrupted.

"Or maybe it's because Candice will be at the table," Emily added.

Michael, normally not one to be shy, looked a little embarrassed. "Well, maybe it's both." He added a grin at Candice for good measure.

Jayden jumped into the conversation right then with exuberance. "Hey, Daddy! Mommy and I will be helping with the doggies and handing out food to dogs who can't eat."

"They don't *have* food to eat," Emily corrected.

Jayden responded, "Yeah, that."

They all laughed.

As the adults sipped on kombucha and margaritas, they talked about the various aspects of the big day. The projects ranged from building storage units to promoting beautification and awareness, food and clothes distribution, tent repair, and more. Jayden began to fade as the conversation continued into the night.

After Chris put Jayden down for bed and read him a story, he came outside to find the patio cleared, the kitchen clean, and the three others getting comfortable around the television. Emily was flipping the remote between Amazon Prime and Netflix.

"We're going to watch *Same Kind of Different as Me*. It's a story about a homeless man in Fort Worth. No one's seen it, and the night is young," Michael said.

"It's a true story," Candice added.

It wasn't long before Emily got up to grab some tissue.

At the end of the emotional movie, everyone was inspired, but tired and ready to call it a night. Michael and Candice went their separate ways, and Emily went to shower while Chris checked on Jayden one more time. Watching his son sleep in the glow of the nightlight always brought peace to Chris's mind and heart. Chris was touched by Jayden's excitement earlier that evening about helping dogs "who can't eat."

Lately he'd started feeling genuinely passionate about the extra hours of work he was investing in the Beyond the Bridge event. It was even more special since Emily and Jayden had also started to share his enthusiasm. And now Michael even seemed willing to help, even if it was just because Candice would be there. Chris smiled at the thought of his family and friends sharing something that was becoming such an important part of his life. He never would have imagined how his life would change just a few months ago. And the best was yet to come.

◆ ◆ ◆

PERSONAL REFLECTION QUESTIONS FOR BOARD MEMBERS

Ask yourself the following questions and journal key points:

» How well do your top 5 friends know, understand, and support the organization you serve?

» How do you leverage your personal strengths, as well as those of your company, to further the goals, mission, and vision of your organization?

» Is there a book or movie that addresses the mission of your organization, like *Same Kind of Different as Me* does for homelessness? If so, how can you use it to learn more and inform others?

GROUP DISCUSSION QUESTIONS FOR BOARD MEMBERS

With a group of other board members, discuss the following questions and note key points:

» How can we learn more about specific organizational needs that we could impact?

» How can we appropriately raise awareness about our organization with friends and family?

» What needs some "mojo" in the coming 6-12 months that could make a difference for our organization?

SUGGESTED ACTIONS FOR BOARD MEMBERS

» **Bronze:** Put a reminder on your calendar or in your pocket this week and seek to tell 10 people about your organization.

» **Silver:** Find a movie that addresses issues that your organization tackles. Watch it with a friend or family member to see if it's worth using for a discussion starter in the future.

» **Gold:** Have discussions with leaders in your company about leveraging company resources to support your community.

SEVEN

Retreat…and Move Forward!

"SO, ARE YOU LOOKING forward to going?"

Emily and Chris were discussing his upcoming board retreat for TCC while doing the dishes after dinner.

"I was!" Chris replied, handing her a cup to dry.

Emily grimaced. "What does that mean?"

"There have been several weird emails this week. First, Roger asked me if I was even going…then he wanted to know if I thought the retreat was required! Can you believe it? Susan also posed some odd questions of both Jennifer and Michelle and copied everyone on the email."

Chris was getting flustered. He did not like conflict in any form.

"What's the purpose of this retreat anyway?" Emily wanted to know.

"Jennifer confessed that they weren't sure of the purpose when they first put it on our calendar. When we joined the board, Jennifer and Michelle gave us all the dates of the board meetings, some major events, and this retreat. As the retreat grew closer, they said they would consider everything going on and determine the agenda then."

"Okay, what do you think needs to happen?" Emily asked patiently, even as she thought, "Get to the point, Chris."

"I think the primary purpose is for us to get to know each other even better. We also need to look at how we can each make the greatest impact."

"What's Susan's issue with that?"

"I'm not sure. There's a chance I'm just reading something into her messages. You know how email can be?"

"That I do," Emily sighed, recalling a miscommunication with one of her nutrition clients that almost cost her the relationship. Fortunately, before it went too far in the wrong direction, she had picked up the phone and asked to meet face to face.

◆

Darius's company had a large conference room on the top floor of their building with plenty of room and magnificent views. It was a perfect choice for hosting the TCC retreat.

When Chris walked into the expansive space, Juan caught Chris's eye and pointed at his chest, cocking his head sideways as if asking a question. Chris had no idea what Juan meant by this gesture. Then Juan moved his lips, as if Chris could read lips, but Chris just shook his head to tell him he couldn't understand.

Juan laughed and came closer. "Where's your pocket square? I've never seen you without one."

Chris grinned and thought how true that was! "It's a retreat, so I decided to be a little more casual."

"Can you work without it?" Juan quipped.

Michelle began the meeting by thanking everyone for giving their time. Everyone was there, except Roger. Michelle explained that he'd had "something come up at work." He would make it to the afternoon segment. Chris didn't know it at the time, but he would never see Roger again. Something always seemed to "come up," and Roger just drifted off.

The facilitator for the retreat was Neal, a tall man with an athletic build and a big smile. Michelle introduced him. "Neal led a session at a conference I attended in Chicago last year. As I was in his breakout session, I thought he was the one who needs to lead our next board retreat! So, please give a big Austin welcome to Neal!"

Neal bounded up to the front and thanked everyone! "Right now," he said, "let's all form a big circle."

Chris looked around the room and saw Jennifer, LaShonda, and Juan quickly taking their places, and he rose swiftly. Meanwhile, Susan had a look on her face that said, "*I can't believe I gave up my Friday to sing kumbaya!*" She slowly rose, straightened her pen and paper, and begrudgingly joined the circle.

"I want you to look around the room at the wonderful people you serve with. Make eye contact with the person you know the least. If they are looking at you, point at each other, and leave the circle." Soon everyone in the room had a partner.

"Now that you're paired up, I want you to find four things that you have in common. And I don't want it to be something like you both live in Texas. Or that you've both eaten at

McDonald's! Go deep and find four intriguing similarities," Neal instructed.

He gave all the pairs time to finish, checking in occasionally. And then he had each couple report their findings.

Juan shared that he and Jennifer both considered their children a huge priority, they loved authentic Mexican food, they started working at a young age, and both liked to get dressed up for special occasions.

Susan went next and made it short and sweet. "Neither LaShonda nor I were born in Texas. We're not big fans of the heat here. We want to make TCC better. And we like big dogs."

When the exercise was over, Neal explained the purpose of the activity. "I'm a firm believer that when you know each other better, you'll make increasingly better decisions for TCC. When we know each other, we build trust. That trust allows us to know when to rely on one another and when to challenge one another. This is a good step already, and we'll sprinkle in opportunities like this one throughout our day. It's my hope that it doesn't stop at the end of the day and that you'll seek ways to know and build relationships with your fellow board members."

Chris wasn't sure, but he thought he saw Susan roll her eyes at this suggestion.

Neal placed everyone in groups of five next. He spread them throughout the room at different tables where he'd set butcher paper and scented markers. Some upbeat music began playing in the background.

"I want your group to draw, yes draw, the current reality for Travis County Cares," Neal instructed. LaShonda and Juan looked at each other, curious as to what was going on.

"I want you to depict both internal and external items," Neal continued. "I'm going to give you about 35 minutes. Please discuss these issues among your group and draw each one as best you can. If necessary, you can use up to five words to add clarity. Also, be sure someone in your group is the spokesperson to share your drawing. Go!"

Susan was in a group with Chris and three long-standing board members.

"I can't believe we're *drawing*!" Susan complained. "Does he think we're five years old?"

Chris ignored Susan's comment. He grabbed a marker, sniffed it enthusiastically to make the others laugh, and said, "Ahh, blueberry! Now, what are some of the current issues and items going on with TCC?"

The group proceeded to talk about the growing homeless population in Austin, including their thoughts about the gentrification happening on the east side of I-35. They felt TCC was a little under-staffed, and they noted that the finances were stable.

Consistently, the more experienced board members in Chris's group spoke from their expertise. Chris was also able to share with confidence what he'd seen and heard first-hand related to the homeless population along the lake. Additionally, he added his opinion on TCC's messaging and social media.

"I think we've done a fair job of getting the word out about TCC, but there's still plenty of opportunities out there to grow," he explained.

Susan quickly replied, "Exactly! I don't think Michelle is pushing our city leaders or doing enough media interviews. If I was the executive director, I'd be the go-to person for homelessness in Austin."

One of the more senior board members responded pointedly, "Do you know what TCC was like before Michelle showed up?"

"No, I don't," Susan answered sharply. "And I'm not sure that I care. I'm responsible for seeing results now. That's why I'm on this board."

With a disarming Texas twang, he replied, "Susan, let's meet for lunch near TCC soon. I'll share a little background that you'll never hear from Michelle and give you insights that just might change your mind."

Susan gave a reluctant nod regarding the meeting that, in her mind, would never happen. The group resumed completing Neal's assignment.

When Neal's timer sounded, every group shared their sketch of the current reality for TCC. One long-time board member spoke up after the exercise. "I'm a little jealous," she said. "These new board members just learned more about TCC than I've known after serving four years. That was so insightful!"

David, the CFO, chimed in, "Well, I work there about 45 hours a week, and I heard some things about our history and current situation that I didn't know. That was awesome!"

Neal then sent everyone out for a 15-minute break.

◆

When everyone was back in the room, Neal asked Michelle to provide the executive director's report on their three-year strategic plan. For the new board members' benefit, Michelle included some information about how the plan had been created. She let everyone know what items had been executed in the previous year and what her leadership team believed needed to be adjusted. Michelle also talked about the main priorities for the coming year, including a few specific items related to the Beyond the Bridge events.

Neal dwarfed Michelle as he stepped up beside her when she finished her update. It was like The Rock standing next to Melissa McCarthy.

"Thanks for that, Michelle. Who has questions for her or any other board member?" Neal asked.

"Did you make the unilateral decision to alter the strategic plan?" Susan wanted to know.

The question was obviously aimed at Michelle.

Jennifer stood up before Michelle could speak. "As we all know, strategic plans are living documents. They must be changed as we gain new information and situations change. Every quarter, the leadership team provides the executive committee with an update. It was there that they proposed the changes, and we agreed. Those updates were provided to the board members who were members at the time."

Michelle was thankful for Jennifer's leadership. Susan had recently taken a very antagonistic tone, both behind closed doors, in emails, and occasionally publicly like this. Michelle had even heard a rumor that morning from another board member that Susan sought to "dethrone her and take her job." Michelle and Jennifer had spoken briefly about this problem at a break earlier in the day. They both knew they would need to address it...and soon.

Jennifer realized from past experience that it was her responsibility to broach the issues with Susan. She'd seen what happens when board dysfunction is allowed to continue. It spreads and ravages an organization like cancer. It hurts board morale, slows down decision making, results in poor attendance at meetings, and causes staff to question their roles. She wouldn't allow that to happen at TCC.

Neal facilitated a few more questions from members, though they were much less challenging in their tone and more informational.

Soon it was time for lunch. "I have assigned you into groups that combine new and long-standing board members," Neal said. "I want you to get to know each other over lunch and discuss what part of the strategic plan is most exciting to you. Enjoy!"

◆

After everyone finished eating, Neal handed out a document to every board member. He encouraged them to take their time answering the following questions:

- What aspect of our current reality at TCC surprised you the most?

- What part of the strategic plan is most exciting to you? Why?

- How do you see yourself making the most impact on the strategic elements of the coming year?

- When your time serving on this board is over, what do you want your legacy to be?

- How can you become an Ambassador and champion for

taking TCC to the next level?

With soothing jazz music playing in the background, all the board members went to work on their answers. Juan finished first and looked around to see the progress of others. LaShonda was barely halfway through when he finished.

"Us lawyers get paid for our words," she said, smiling at Juan.

"People like their construction projects done on time," Juan retorted with a bigger grin.

"We work at different paces and bring a great level of diversity to the board," Neal reminded everyone. "That's what makes us a great board!"

Michelle liked his inclusive language. His mannerisms and word choice made him seem like one of them.

Everyone got back to the task at hand as Neal continued to walk around the room, looking over shoulders to see what had been written. He read Juan's answers first since he was finished and skimmed several others. As the last board members finished the assignment, he reflected on this group. "They are an exceptional board. They have diversity in strengths, industry, personality, race, and gender. Plus, they're so engaged and open to learning." But, he told himself, he had to talk to Michelle about Susan. There was something wrong there, and she did not seem like a fit. Susan had cornered Neal during one of the breaks, and he sensed she was trouble.

Once everyone finished, Neal wanted them to partner with someone they'd not yet been with to discuss the answers to the first two questions. Any inhibitions that were present in the morning sessions were gone by now. Everyone jumped in with enthusiasm, except Susan. She was clearly resisting.

Neal had presented all day, but he still delivered the next set of instructions with the energy of Buddy the Elf. "Now I want you to share the answers to the next three questions as if you were at our board retreat one year from now. For example, I might say, 'I was able to make significant introductions to three key people that resulted in TCC receiving $300,000 in donations and grants!'"

Michelle let out a whoop and said, "Now, we're talking, Neal!" Everyone laughed. Even Susan.

The room was soon buzzing. Neal had the group switch partners and repeat the answers. He walked around the room to ensure everyone had the opportunity to talk, and then he moved them on to their next facilitated activity to keep the momentum going.

After the afternoon break, the new development director at TCC provided an update and sought input from the board members. It was clear that more conversations would be needed about how the board members could "open doors" to more grants and donors.

Next, Neal led a session that helped board members brainstorm the specific people, foundations, and donors needed to connect with TCC. He also prompted them to think about other ways to help fundraise.

Chris was shocked that he hadn't previously thought about asking his parents about foundations that might be sympathetic to homelessness. He also had not even considered if Sharp Edge could do some corporate matching for gifts. He'd have to talk to Jennifer about that. One of his and Emily's favorite restaurants also had a monthly opportunity to give back to local nonprofits.

He could easily talk to the manager about TCC. "How could I have missed those opportunities?" he wondered.

Neal concluded his talk and nodded at Jennifer, signaling he was finished.

"Let's all thank Neal for facilitating a great board retreat," Jennifer said.

There was a lot of clapping, smiling, and nodding. "I want to thank you for your service and for giving your time, talents, and treasure!" Again, the room erupted in applause.

"And, I'd like us all to thank our fearless leader, Michelle, for another successful year and a great year to come!" Again, the room burst into applause, minus Susan who gathered her things to leave. Jennifer concluded, "Our retreat is adjourned. Have a fabulous weekend with your family!"

Chris high-fived Juan as he headed out the door, ready to spend time with Jayden and Emily. Twenty minutes later, while Michelle was stopped at a traffic light, she saw a text pop up from Jennifer.

**I will address the Susan
issue next week.**

Michelle replied before the light turned green.

Let me know what you need from me.

Michelle sighed. This was going to be interesting.

Let's talk Monday!

❖ ❖ ❖

PERSONAL REFLECTION QUESTIONS FOR BOARD MEMBERS

Ask yourself the following questions and journal key points:

» How have you seen fellow board members use their unique skills, experience, and relationships to further your organization?

» How can *you* increasingly use your skills, experience, and relationships to further your organization?

» If your board hosted a retreat, what elements would be important to cover this year?

GROUP DISCUSSION QUESTIONS FOR BOARD MEMBERS

With a group of other board members, discuss the following questions and note key points:

» What is the current reality, internally and externally, for our organization?

» How would you articulate the strategic initiatives or goals of our organization for the coming year?

» What would you like your legacy to be after your board service is over?

SUGGESTED ACTIONS FOR BOARD MEMBERS

» **Bronze:** Make notes of what strengths each board member brings to your board.

» **Silver:** Take the time to discover and understand which initiatives will make the greatest impact in your organization for the coming year.

» **Gold:** Actively help to coordinate the strategic planning and/or retreat process for your organization.

EIGHT

Stepping Up!

IT WAS THE STRAW that broke the camel's back. Jennifer waited anxiously as the board members began arriving one by one at TCC. She had some news to share, and she wasn't entirely sure how it would go over.

To Chris, it seemed as if the next board meeting snuck up on him rather quickly. Today, the schedule allowed for an hour longer than usual to accommodate a training session after they completed their regular board meeting agenda. Michelle had explained that they would use this session to brainstorm the roles and responsibilities of a board member.

This time, Chris came prepared for the meeting and felt a bit more confident. He was thankful to see his table tent name card was next to LaShonda.

"Do we have a quorum?" Jennifer asked, calling the meeting to order.

Michelle started counting heads. "We do, in fact. Everyone is here."

"Not everyone. Susan isn't here," Natalie observed as she looked around the room.

Jennifer wished she could tell the whole story about a series of concerning issues, culminating in Susan going around Michelle's back and trying to drive a wedge between Michelle and the CFO. When she met with Susan to discuss her difficult behavior and the negative impact it was having, Susan was furious. Jennifer spoke kindly and asked questions to try to understand why Susan was behaving the way she was. She had found in past situations that sometimes people just need to feel heard, so she intended to give Susan that opportunity. The approach didn't work well though, and Susan only became more irate and irrational as the conversation progressed. Jennifer had to expedite ending the meeting by letting Susan know she should submit a request to resign from her position as a board member to avoid action by the governance committee. It was not how Jennifer had hoped the conversation would end, but she felt she had no choice.

"That is actually one of the announcements I have for today. Susan has decided that this board isn't the right fit for her, and she has resigned."

"That's a good thing, I think," LaShonda said boldly. "After the retreat, I even wondered if TCC was the right place for me because of how uncomfortable Susan made it for all of us. I don't need that negativity."

A few board members nodded in solidarity, but Jennifer felt it was best not to verbally agree and vowed to avoid speaking negatively about Susan.

However, Michelle added in a comment that Jennifer appreciated. "LaShonda, I want you to know that we recognized what was going on at the retreat. Here's the thing. It's okay if all of us don't agree on everything. In fact, we need that. However, what is important is that we can ask questions, listen, and be respectful when we disagree. As the executive director, I want to make sure we maintain a culture that expects respectful communication."

"We appreciate that, and thank you for considering the importance of board culture," LaShonda responded.

Jennifer knew they had made the right decision to address the issues with Susan. She didn't like doing it, but she knew it was part of her responsibility as board chair.

There was a different air in the room today with Susan's absence. The board meeting ran smoothly. In fact, it was one of their better ones as board members were actively engaged in rich discussions that provided the staff with some helpful ideas.

When they had covered all the topics on the agenda, Jennifer and Michelle launched into the special board training segment.

"So, let's start by hearing your perspectives," Jennifer stated. "In your opinion, what are your roles and responsibilities as a board member?" Jennifer captured their ideas on the whiteboard:

- Attend board meetings

- Participate in the meetings

- Serve on at least one committee

- Give financially to TCC

- Connect TCC to finances

- Be a positive representative for TCC

Jennifer stopped after writing the last item. "What does that mean? What does a positive representative look like?"

"I think it means being a voice for TCC and the people it serves whenever we can. It's being a cheerleader for the cause we serve...like being an Ambassador of TCC," Leah suggested.

"An Ambassador," Michelle repeated slowly. "Let's explore this a bit more. Someone look up that word."

Juan must have already been searching online because he spoke up quickly, reading the definition from his phone. "An ambassador is a person who acts as a representative or promoter of a specific group or activity."

Everyone sat quietly for a moment, letting the definition sink in. "What words stand out to you?" Jennifer asked.

"A promoter," Chris threw in. "I haven't thought of it that way. All of the things we came up with so far are tactical...attend the meetings, be on a committee, etc. But being a promoter seems like a whole other level."

"So, what would we need to do to be Ambassadors?" Jennifer prompted.

"Well, when I think of being a promoter, I think of speaking to others about the organization to build awareness. I'm not super comfortable speaking, though, so maybe I'm not a good promoter," Juan admitted.

"I agree and disagree with you, Juan," Chris said. "I agree that a promoter is one who speaks to others, but I disagree that you don't promote." Chris had often seen Juan promoting TCC through their work together on the Beyond the Bridge committee. "You may not be presenting to companies about our work or attending events as a public speaker, but I hear you promoting TCC to your crews and vendors. And you are always speaking out about what you feel is best for the homeless. You are an Ambassador for sure!"

"I hadn't thought of it that way. Thanks, Chris," Juan beamed.

"I like the way you are all thinking!" Jennifer said, looking to continue focusing the conversation. "What other examples have you seen of each other being an Ambassador for TCC?"

"I have a question. At the last board meeting, you recognized LaShonda for sharing TCC posts on social media. I don't use Facebook. Is that an expectation of us?" Juan asked.

Chris nodded in agreement. He'd wondered the same thing.

"Well, what do you all think? Is it an expectation of all board members to use social media to promote TCC?" Michelle asked of the group.

LaShonda shared her thoughts. "I guess we all have various strengths and talents, so we all can be Ambassadors in different ways. I think that if someone has social media, it would be a good practice to share posts and comment as much as possible. But I'm not sure it should be expected that board members who don't use social media have to get accounts."

The group continued to have a robust conversation about what it means to be an Ambassador. After about 15 minutes of discussion, they had created a list of the actions Ambassadors can take:

- Ongoing recruitment of board members, donors, and volunteers

- Volunteering for various events and meeting volunteer needs

- Connecting your company in some way (such as utilizing talents, skills, and resources)
- Proactively sharing and posting on social media
- Proactively sharing information with colleagues, friends, and family
- Fundraising both for formal events and ongoing efforts through personal connections
- Connecting your strengths, knowledge, and talents with TCC's needs
- Networking with others and making connections to TCC
- Speaking on behalf of TCC at engagements when possible
- Building awareness about topics or events that matter to TCC

Jennifer agreed to type up their list and share it via email later. She reminded them of TCC's own Ambassador Award, as well as the mayor's citywide emphasis. "This is a great list. Here's our final question of the day. What do you need from us to be equipped and fulfill these roles and responsibilities?"

"Public speaking classes," Juan teased. "In all seriousness, each of us may need different things, depending on our skills and knowledge. I would need public speaking classes for sure, but Chris probably wouldn't need that! Maybe we can come up with a general list that all of us will likely need." Juan suggested they make talking points to follow when sharing information about TCC.

"Thanks for the kudos, Juan," Chris responded. "Yes, talking points would be super helpful. Some great stories would also be nice to have. Remember Scott from our first training? I bet we all remember his story. There are probably many stories out there we could share when appropriate. Stories are so powerful."

The group continued suggesting ideas for what they needed:

- Stories that get to the heart from each of our programs

- Talking points that can be used with groups and individuals

- Collateral such as brochures, email flyers, and social media posts to share

- Lists of potential donors for cultivation

- Opportunities to speak and share

- Details about various volunteering and networking opportunities

Michelle played a short video about using the back of a napkin at lunch to guide a simple, meaningful conversation about TCC to help someone visually understand more about TCC's work. The board members all agreed that it was 10 minutes well spent.

Again, Jennifer told the group that she would send all the notes to them and thanked them for their hard work during the training.

It was at that moment that Chris looked at his phone and saw three missed calls from Emily. That's odd, he thought, and checked his texts. There weren't any from his wife. Just then, his phone screen lit up with a call from Emily's number.

He took the call, walking into the hallway for privacy.

"Emily?" he said, a hint of concern in his voice.

A man's voice started to speak.

"Who are you? Why are you on my wife's phone?" Chris barked.

"Sir, do you have a son named Jayden?"

Chris was visibly shaken. "Yes, of course. Why do you have my wife's phone? What's going on?"

"Sir, please calm down and listen. I'm only trying to help," the voice from Emily's phone insisted. "Your wife and son have been struck by a car in a crosswalk. Your son is going to be fine."

"What about Emily?" Chris yelled, steadying himself against the wall with his free hand. He listened one minute more, hung up the phone, and paced madly without saying a word.

The other board members heard Chris's distress and came out into the hallway to support him. Jennifer grabbed a chair and encouraged Chris to sit. He refused and continued to pace. Juan grabbed a glass of water and briefly put a hand on Chris's shoulder before Chris bolted for the door.

◆ ◆ ◆

PERSONAL REFLECTION QUESTIONS FOR BOARD MEMBERS

Ask yourself the following questions and journal key points:

» When was the last time you performed each of the Ambassador roles and responsibilities outlined in this chapter?

» Which three Ambassador roles and responsibilities align best with your skills and strengths?

» How can you be an Ambassador during the next 90 days?

» Do you have the tools you need to be equipped to be an Ambassador? If not, what do you need?

GROUP DISCUSSION QUESTIONS FOR BOARD MEMBERS

With a group of other board members, discuss the following questions and note key points:

» How would we define the culture of our board? (Not the culture of the organization.)

» What do we encourage and celebrate at the board level?

» What do we discourage and correct at the board level?

» Do we compliment and complement each other well?

SUGGESTED ACTIONS FOR BOARD MEMBERS

» **Bronze:** Make some notes in your phone about key stories and facts about your organization.

» **Silver:** Create one or more documents using this information to share with other board members.

» **Gold:** Make a presentation using these key stories and facts to a potential donor/volunteer who could benefit the organization if they were more aware of its work. Invite another board member to join you.

NINE

When Conflicts Arise

THE NEXT FEW DAYS were a blur. The phone call at TCC was a terrifying moment that Chris would never forget. Every time Chris thought about the accident and what could have happened, he was both anxious and thankful. Jayden was in much better condition than Emily, with just some bruised ribs and minor abrasions. Emily was very hurt, but she was expected to make a full recovery.

The police report cited several witnesses who claimed that Emily had been given the pedestrian signal to proceed across the street. Still, the distracted driver had been looking at their phone and treated the red light as a stop sign, pausing only briefly before accelerating into Emily.

His wife's quick thinking had shielded Jayden from greater harm, although she took the brunt of the force. Emily's maternal instincts were extraordinary, and she somehow lifted Jayden up off the ground just before impact. The police officers and emergency personnel at the scene were shocked that Emily had reacted quickly enough to take any action at all.

Chris kept trying to put out of his mind what could have resulted if Emily had not shown super-human abilities. He needed to shake those thoughts out of his head, but they seemed to overwhelm him and consume his dreams even when he slept.

While there is never a good time for such a tragic event, Chris often thought about the accident's terrible timing. The Beyond the Bridge event was fast approaching. Chris had to trust the committee to pick up the pieces that he left unfinished. Emily and Jayden needed his complete focus.

When the big day arrived, the fact that he wasn't there ate at Chris. Jennifer wasn't surprised when she saw his name pop up on her phone later that morning as she rushed around City Life Church. The church was conveniently located on 3rd street downtown near the rest of the day's activities. The leaders had graciously offered their facilities to serve as the hub for the Beyond the Bridge events.

"Hey, Chris! How are Emily and Jayden doing?"

"They're still making good progress. Again, we're so grateful they will recover. It could have been so much worse," Chris said, sensing the familiar ominous feeling again as he talked about the accident.

"Yes, we are all so glad to hear that." It was a relief to get a positive update on Chris's family to share with the rest of the board members.

"Thanks for picking up the phone," Chris said. "I know it's a crazy busy day for you. Again, I'm so sorry I can't be there to see it all in action."

"No apology needed! There is no other place you should be! And don't worry about us. You and the committee had things so well planned that the execution is the easy part. Your committee's detailed notes and planning documents were a lifesaver. Everything is going smoothly so far."

Chris wished he could be in two places at once and see for himself the hundreds of people who cared enough to show up and help their fellow citizens. "What's happening so far?" he wanted to know, pressing for more details.

Jennifer spent a few minutes telling Chris about the bustling activity of the day. A group of volunteers with sewing experience had just left the church to head out to various areas to repair tents. Another group of veterinary professionals were immunizing and spaying animals belonging to the homeless. Volunteers were busy giving the dogs baths and handing out pet food.

When he heard this, Chris thought about how Emily and Jayden had planned to volunteer at this station for Beyond the Bridge. Jayden had such a soft spot for animals, and his son had been looking forward to helping animals in need.

"Hundreds of other volunteers are spread out across the city to help," Jennifer explained.

Even though Chris couldn't be there, pride swelled up inside his heart. All his hard work had been worth it. "If you see Juan, give him my thanks. He has been a rock star."

Michael happened to be working alongside Candice at the volunteer check-in table at the church and overheard Jennifer talking to Chris. Chris heard Michael say, "Hey, Jennifer. Tell him that we have it all covered. Candice and I will stop by later tonight with dinner."

Michael and Candice had become great friends since eating dinner at Chris and Emily's house six months ago. Unlike previous relationships, Michael seemed to enjoy simple activities with Candice, like feeding the ducks at the lake and sharing a picnic on the balcony of his condo. Candice had made it clear to Michael early in their friendship that she was not one to jump into a relationship lightly. But Michael seemed genuinely happy just spending time with her and letting the friendship grow.

A few days before the accident, Michael and Candice had joined Chris and Emily again for dinner. Chris and Emily both noticed the sweet glances the two shared. It was apparent their friendship was evolving into something more. There was a time when Chris would have cringed at the thought of Michael pursuing another relationship, but Michael had changed in so many ways recently. He was genuinely happy about volunteering for Beyond the Bridge, and not just because it would mean more time with Candice!

"Hey, Chris, get back to caring for your family. A group of construction volunteers just arrived. Thanks for calling to make sure we were all in line this morning," Jennifer said.

"It's just great to be a part of it in some small way," Chris began before Jennifer interrupted him.

"Oh, you are part of this in a big way! Just because you can't be here today does not minimize the huge role you played in making this a success."

Chris thanked Jennifer. As he hung up the phone, he felt exhilarated and sad at the same time. He could tell in Jennifer's voice that Beyond the Bridge was going well, even if he couldn't be there in person. Chris put his phone in his pocket and walked down the hallway toward Emily's hospital room.

Emily was just waking up as he entered. It was exhausting for her with the nurses filing in and out of the room at all hours.

Emily did her best to sleep when she could. It was difficult to see his wife in so much pain. The impact broke her shoulder and several ribs, and she had numerous lacerations requiring stitches.

The doctors said her shoulder surgery went well, and she would start physical therapy soon. The hospital wanted to keep Emily to monitor her, which left Chris in a sticky situation. He wanted to spend as much time with Emily as possible, but Jayden also needed him at home.

"Hey, any word on how Beyond the Bridge is going today?" Emily asked sleepily.

"Yes, I just got off the phone with Jennifer, and it sounds like the day is off to a great start."

"Of course, it is! How could it not go well? All of the hard work over the past few months will make today spectacular."

"I hope you are right. Let's get to the most important topic. Did you get some sleep?"

"I slept some, I think. I don't remember what time the nurse came in last, but it was probably at the shift change around 6:00. I have been asleep since then."

"Well, that's better than nothing. What is on the agenda for the day? Spin class? Yoga? A bike ride around the neighborhood?" Chris teased sweetly.

"I wish. How about just getting my hair washed?"

"I can do better than that! I watched a YouTube video on how to give a DIY pedicure," Chris said, pulling out a small box of supplies. "Today, you will not only get your hair washed, but you will have a pedicure complete with your favorite polish color—Sunset Wish."

"Really? Wow, this should be interesting!" Emily exclaimed,

just as the shift nurse entered the room. April had been Emily's nurse a few times since Emily moved out of the ICU a few days ago, and Chris appreciated her personal care and concern.

"What's that?" April inquired, pointing to the polish.

"Chris has prepared a spa day for me," Emily answered.

"I have four daughters, so I have had some practice painting toenails if you need help, Chris," April offered.

He smiled and delighted in the small wins. Life was unpredictable, but the twists and turns were giving him perspective on what is important. He held Emily's hand as April began her routine checks of IVs and vitals. He could tell by looking into Emily's eyes that she felt blessed in the same way.

◆

In true kid form, Jayden seemed to be bouncing back very quickly. The hospital had kept him for two days of observation, but everything else seemed to check out. Neighbors and soccer families had been spoiling him with his favorite foods and plenty of entertainment. His best buddy's mom, Kelsey, had been staying with Jayden during the day to allow Chris time with Emily. Kelsey was an ER doctor who worked sporadically, so she was a huge help in many ways.

After Chris finished the spa day and helped Emily with lunch, he headed back home to see Jayden. He debated calling Juan on the drive to find out how the various construction projects were going but decided against it.

"Maybe I'll call Juan tomorrow," Chris decided, even though he wanted to talk to him right then.

Suddenly his phone began to ring. He took it out of his

pocket. It was Juan!

"Hey, I was just thinking of calling you!"

"That's funny. I just finished lunch, and didn't want to bother you, but I had to tell you how well things are going! In fact, we are ahead of schedule on a few projects. The new clothes closet build-out is complete, and the paint crew should head there soon. The shelves at the Riverside Food Pantry are finished. I have a crew going back in a few days to restock the shelves once the paint is dry."

"You are the man!" Chris said.

"Nope, it took all of us. Everyone is so excited to help! I'm especially proud of the employees on my team who are volunteering today. You should see the pride in their eyes to be able to serve others. Some of them have been on the receiving end needing help. Being able to pay it forward is something they will never forget."

Chris suddenly thought back to the company announcement last fall and Jennifer's prediction that they would receive benefits from volunteering. At the time, he'd wondered what she was talking about. In this moment, though, it became clear.

"Juan, it is so great to hear how your team stepped up to help and that they are feeling good about helping others," Chris said.

Juan was even considering implementing something like Sharp Edge did, asking his employees to spend paid time volunteering. "I'm not sure we will be able to manage all the time that Sharp Edge allows, but I know we can do something. Maybe employees can take eight hours to volunteer each year, and we will pay them so they don't have to take vacation time to do it."

"That's a great idea, Juan!"

Juan then asked Chris for a quick update on Emily and Jayden.

"I'm glad that she is making progress. My boys drew some pictures and wrote some notes for Jayden. Do you mind if we stop by tomorrow after work to deliver them? Let me know what his favorite flavor of ice cream is, and we will make sure we bring that."

"Aw, man. That would be great," Chris replied. The two friends hung up. Chris was in awe of how life-changing this year had been for him and for Juan.

◆ ◆ ◆

PERSONAL REFLECTION QUESTIONS FOR BOARD MEMBERS

Ask yourself the following questions and journal key points:

» Do you ever feel torn between board duties and personal responsibilities? If so, how do you manage the situation?

» Has serving on a board changed your life in any way? How so?

» Would you recommend serving on a board to other people? Why or why not?

» Do you have a preferred way of introducing others to your organization? Explain.

GROUP DISCUSSION QUESTIONS FOR BOARD MEMBERS

With a group of other board members, discuss the following questions and note key points:

» How does our organization encourage us to engage others in our cause?

» How could we raise the level of awareness for our cause in our community?

» What could we do to encourage more corporate engagement with our nonprofit?

» How aware are our civic leaders about our organization? What could we do to help them be more aware? What benefits could that reap?

SUGGESTED ACTIONS FOR BOARD MEMBERS

» **Bronze:** Write a note to fellow board members facing adversity or celebrating a milestone.

» **Silver:** Look for ways to engage more community members in giving back and serving with your organization.

» **Gold:** Discuss with your executive director and board chair about a much-needed event or project that hasn't had a champion. Be the champion!

TEN

The Ambassador

"I CAN'T BELIEVE IT'S still so hot here!" Chris's mother said emphatically.

"Blimey hot, I'd say," Chris's father added with a terrible attempt at a British accent.

They arrived on a Wednesday afternoon in late October to visit Chris and his family. He picked them up at Austin-Bergstrom International Airport with Jayden in tow.

"Snow cones would make us cool again!" Jayden took the opportunity to suggest. And so, in typical grandparenting fashion, the family drove to Jayden's favorite snow cone vendor called Artic Ice.

Chris worked during the day at the office and entertained his parents during the evenings. Emily took advantage of the extra hands and gave her doting in-laws some special time with Jayden. That way she could leave the house to have coffee with friends and do her physical therapy.

Chris had shared with Emily several months earlier that

TCC was set to receive an award at the upcoming Mayor's Community Impact Initiative dinner, and all board members were asked to attend. She was happy to join him, which Chris appreciated. When Chris had told his parents about the dinner falling during their visit, his father had offered a solution.

"Buy a couple of extra tickets to the event, and I'll pay you back. It will be interesting to see what other communities are doing," he'd suggested.

Chris, of course, deflected the financial offer and said he'd cover the cost. He was completely clueless that Emily had been working in the background to ensure Chris's parents were in town for the Mayor's dinner.

Friday night finally arrived. Chris had encouraged Emily to stay home, but she wouldn't have it. "Afraid I'll slow you down?" she quipped. While she didn't have the stamina she'd had before the accident, her recovery was coming along remarkably.

During the social hour, Chris was pleased to introduce his parents to Michelle, Jennifer, Juan, LaShonda, and several other board members and staff from TCC. Surprisingly, even Michael was there, with Candice, no less.

Chris introduced his parents to Michael. "This is my number one running buddy and good friend, Michael, and Emily's good friend, Candice. Well, she's my friend, too," he laughed. Candice feigned a hurt look before smiling.

After the six of them chatted a while, Chris said under his breath to Michael, "I'm surprised to see you here."

"Hey, it's a great networking opportunity! Plus, it's a nice way to spend some time with Candice!" he said with a wink. Chris shook his head and grinned, shuffling his parents off to their seats at the TCC table.

As the evening proceeded, several organizations received awards and accolades for their accomplishments for making Austin a better place. Much to Chris's surprise, TCC had not received any recognition yet. Nervously, he straightened his pocket square and then checked his phone to be sure there were no messages from the babysitter. He looked at his parents, who seemed enthralled to hear what was going on to help those less fortunate in the Austin area. He even saw his dad tear up at one point.

Then, the speaker, Don Faxon, was introduced. Chris had not previously heard of Don but was intrigued to hear that he was part of a nationwide network of homeless shelters. Don told story after story of lives changed through their myriad of rescue missions and homeless shelters. He explained how people came in for a free meal, but ended up having their lives transformed, knocking down the barriers of bad behavior and addiction.

It was an inspiring speech, and Chris looked at Jennifer and mouthed, "Thank you!" to her. He couldn't be more pleased to be a part of something that was bigger than himself. Don concluded his message with a challenge to step up and be a part of making a difference for those needing a helping hand.

As Don started to walk off the stage, the mayor stopped him and said, "Don, please stand with me for a minute. As you know, we have a large and growing population of homeless people in Austin. While they do create issues and challenges, they are our citizens, too. Tonight, I want to present our Ambassador Award to a man who has come alongside this population and helped provide food, shelter, dignity, rehab, and a chance for them to reenter our society as contributing members. Don, this man has been a big part of doing everything you shared through your stories."

Don smiled and stepped back as the mayor took some notes out of his jacket pocket to begin reading. "Every year since I've been elected, I have presented the Ambassador Award to a recipient who was nominated by a nonprofit for making a great impact. This year, our award recipient comes to us from Travis County Cares, TCC as many of us know it." He paused.

Emily and Chris's parents fought the urge to look at Chris. Michael was beaming. Michelle was tearing up. Juan and LaShonda were grinning from ear to ear. Jennifer looked straight ahead, staring at the back of Chris's head. Chris was still clueless.

The mayor went on to talk about the fantastic impact TCC was making among the homeless in Travis County and Austin specifically. He told the story of André, who had come to Austin three years prior in hopes of finding a better life but did not immediately discover it. Then, the mayor said, André found a place of refuge at TCC and began making progress toward his goals. The mayor spoke of the recent success of Beyond the Bridge, where countless Austin area residents had learned how to improve the conditions for all who live in Austin.

"Tonight's recipient of the Ambassador Award," he continued, "provides stellar leadership on the board of TCC and relentlessly promotes the good work that TCC does in our community. And if you know him, you've probably already been asked to contribute financially to this worthy cause." The audience chuckled before the mayor added, "While he has done a lot for TCC, he's also taught other organizations how to promote their events and causes through a training he has facilitated at

United Way. Additionally, many of his colleagues at Sharp Edge have used his model at the nonprofits where they serve."

At that point, Michelle took the stage alongside Don. "Tonight, I want to recognize this year's recipient of the Ambassador Award, Chris Stevens." The crowd stood as Chris stared in unbelief. Emily gave him a big hug.

His dad shook him out of his stupor with a friendly punch on the shoulder. "Son, they're waiting for you!"

Chris stood up and slowly walked to the stage, still in shock. This was a moment he could not have imagined just 15 months earlier. Michael and Candice gave him a smile and a thumbs up.

Once on stage, Michelle and Don looped a medallion around Chris's neck that read, "The Ambassador."

Chris, his mind racing, put his public speaking training and experience to good use. He quickly thought back to what he'd learned in his Dale Carnegie communication course.

"First of all, thank you, Mr. Mayor. I love what you're doing to highlight nonprofits who are making such a difference. Don, thank you for your work around the country to re-assimilate those who have found themselves on the receiving side of some challenging situations. I love that you're spearheading a movement! Michelle, thanks for caring for the homeless in our area and helping guide some sometimes-reluctant board members to make a difference. Thanks to my colleague, Jennifer, who nearly forced me into what has now become a labor of love and helped me look beyond my own navel."

The crowd all laughed. His parents looked at each other with big smiles and a few tears.

Chris continued, "Thanks to my wife, Emily, who has patiently encouraged, challenged and supported me to be a part of something bigger than myself. And, thanks to my parents whom I believed until three minutes ago had randomly chosen this date to come for a visit! Thanks, Mom and Dad, for laying a foundation of service that for many years I did not even see."

Chris looked at the audience before him. "And thanks to all of you who make a difference each and every day in your own way at the organizations you serve. You volunteer, you lead, you seek donations, you make connections, you provide your wisdom and expertise, and because of that, you make Austin... which may always be a little weird...a better place! Thank you! I'm humbled and honored to be an Ambassador for Travis County Cares!"

Many with eyes a little moist stood up and gave a standing ovation while Chris walked back to his seat.

As he sat down, Chris was surprised to see Scott, André, and many other current and former clients from Travis County Cares begin to hand out a small gift to everyone seated at the tables.

"Several clients of TCC are handing each of you a coin with 'Be an Ambassador Today' engraved on it," the mayor explained as the men and women made their way through the room. "It is my hope that you will seek opportunities to engage in the life and welfare of others, being an Ambassador for them in the special ways that only you can. Place the coin in your pocket or in a special spot as a reminder that we can all make a difference and be an Ambassador." He paused. "Thank you for coming tonight. Go, and be an Ambassador, just like Chris."

Jennifer and her husband, James, gave Chris a hug and a handshake respectively. Many people whom Chris didn't know came over to congratulate and thank him. Michelle whispered in his ear, "Your parents and Michael have both given significant donations in light of your award, by the way."

Michael and Candice walked over with smiles and gave him a congratulatory hug.

"I hear you made a donation. I'd like to talk more about that and say thank you later. I love 'ya, bro'!" Chris said to Michael.

"You've come a long way, baby!" Michael said and jabbed him in the ribs. Then Michael and Candice headed off for a night of dancing as the band struck up a tune.

Emily, Chris, and his parents eventually headed back to the house. Jayden was still up, albeit past his bedtime.

"Jayden, come here. I want you to see what your dad got tonight," Emily said. She handed him the award, which to nobody's surprise, the boy hung around his neck immediately. "Your daddy got this medal for being such a great man and for being such a good friend to some special people who need our help."

"Yay, Daddy!" Jayden responded, giving Chris a hug.

Chris's dad pulled out the smaller coin that he carried in his pocket and looked at it while he spoke. "It is quite an honor, son, and a great example for many. I'll keep this in my pocket as a reminder."

"I'm not sure you need a reminder, Dad," Chris said. "I think you and Mom were my role models. I'm just sorry I didn't seem to notice or care back then."

Chris's mom jumped in, "Wait until I tell my girlfriends about this!" Chris knew she'd likely already texted some of them in the car on the way home. "I don't know if I'm going to be able to sleep tonight," she added.

"You're being awfully quiet over there," Chris said to his wife.

"I'm just soaking it all in. I'm so proud of you and happy for TCC...and exhausted."

"In hindsight, it seems highly suspicious that my parents would be in town on this exact weekend," Chris said as he furrowed his brow.

"Let's just say that a little birdie—or a great board chair—might have fed me a little information," Emily said with a grin.

Chris shook his head.

"Can I wear this to bed?" Jayden inquired, holding the medal.

"Of course you can, son."

"I'll come in and take it off you once you fall asleep," Emily explained. She then told Jayden to give everyone hugs and kisses before she put him to bed. They were all on quite a high. Chris's parents took advantage of the transition and excused themselves.

"It's been quite a day, and I'm dog-tired," Chris's dad said as they headed off to the guest room.

Chris went back to give Jayden another kiss before retiring. Later, as he laid in bed with his arm tucked around his wife, he thought back to the events of the last year. He reflected on that fateful day when he'd received a meeting request for a last-minute Friday afternoon meeting. It had been a lot of work, but he did love this new aspect to his life. He thoroughly enjoyed the opportunity to use his gifts, talents, treasure, and relationships to help others. Just as Jennifer had predicted, he'd learned a lot and had seen benefits well beyond what he could imagine. It didn't hurt knowing how proud Emily was of him. He pulled her a little closer and kissed the top of her head. She had already fallen asleep and didn't respond.

Chris gingerly slipped his arm out from under her head and rolled over to his side. The last thought he had before falling asleep was, "I wonder what's next?"

❖ ❖ ❖

PERSONAL REFLECTION QUESTIONS FOR BOARD MEMBERS

Ask yourself the following questions and journal key points:

» What stood out to you from this chapter?

» If you were to receive The Ambassador Award, what would they recognize you for achieving?

» If you were to receive The Ambassador Award one year from now, what accomplishments would you want to see recognized related to the impact you made at your organization?

GROUP DISCUSSION QUESTIONS FOR BOARD MEMBERS

With a group of other board members, discuss the following questions and note key points:

» Who stands out on our board as an Ambassador?

» How does our organization show appreciation for those who step up in an exceptional way?

» What outcomes might we see if every board member was an Ambassador?

» How could we encourage that level of commitment to make a greater impact?

SUGGESTED ACTIONS FOR BOARD MEMBERS

» **Bronze:** Make a point to recognize other board members when they step up to a new level of commitment.

» **Silver:** Take an action this week that will increase the recognition of your organization in a meaningful way.

» **Gold:** Sit down with key leaders of your organization to learn more about the greatest needs. Then, go through all your contacts via social media and your contact list to consider who might come alongside your organization to make a difference.

Epilogue

EMILY POURED CHRIS A chai and asked, "Are you nervous?"

He smiled. "To be honest, a little." He sighed and took a sip. "It's not that I don't think I know what to do. Jennifer set a good example, and I've been reading some articles. I feel like Michelle and I will be fine. I think it's the unknown and the situations that will come up at TCC or in the city that I've just not dealt with before."

"You'll do great! I'm sure of it," Emily encouraged. "But, if you don't get out the door with Jayden, he's going to be late to school."

At that point, Jayden walked in with his backpack on and his shirt on backwards.

"Are you going to go in reverse today?" Chris asked. Jayden looked at him confused. Emily kneeled down and whispered, "Your shirt is on backwards, silly." She helped him make it right.

"Bye Mom, bye Baby," Jayden shouted as he headed for the door.

Chris grinned, said his goodbyes, and kissed Emily as he patted her bulging belly.

◆

Once Chris was at the office, he checked his email and reviewed his calendar and email and followed up on the progress of a few projects. Then he stood up and straightened his new pocket square with the TCC logo on it. It had been an unexpected gift from Juan. He smiled. He was grateful for their friendship—one more unexpected benefit of his board service. He walked into several offices, asking questions of colleagues to check on projects. Then he picked up a Coke Zero in the break room. Preston was there, pouring an enormous cup of coffee.

"Check you out! I like that square," Preston boomed. "What's the occasion?"

"Today is my first meeting as board chair. I thought it was fitting," Chris responded.

"Dude! That's great. Jennifer would be proud. Does she know?"

"She knows I'm due to be board chair at TCC, but she doesn't know today is our first board meeting of the year," Chris answered. He paused and gazed into the corner of the break room. "I think I'll go give her a call."

Preston gave him a high-five as they went their separate ways.

"Tell her I said hey," Preston called over his shoulder.

◆

Jennifer answered on the third ring. "Well, this is a pleasant surprise. To what do I owe the pleasure?" Jennifer had taken a job opportunity in Atlanta, Georgia, and Chris had recently followed in her footsteps as board chair at TCC.

"How's it going in Atlanta?" Chris asked.

"It's great, really. I miss you guys, but work is going well. James and I are trying to figure out this empty nest thing. About every other weekend, we're taking trips to explore the area."

"What's been your favorite so far?"

"Savannah," she said without a moment of hesitation. "Ever been?"

"No, but we'll add it to the list."

"Maybe once the baby is born James and I can meet the *four* of you there." She put an emphasis on "four."

"How's Sharp Edge doing?"

"You are certainly missed, but business is strong, and everyone is doing well. Preston says to tell you hello...and to give blood in Atlanta!" He grinned.

"Ha ha. How's TCC?"

"That's the reason I'm calling," Chris said, gazing over downtown Austin. Lady Bird Lake was off to his right.

She interrupted. "What's wrong?"

"No, no, nothing is wrong. But today I chair my first board meeting. Any advice?"

"Oh, Chris, you'll do great."

"You did such a good job as chair, and I think Darius did a great job after you. He advanced some initiatives," Chris offered. "Do you have time for this conversation?"

"Absolutely!" she said. "So, what makes a great board chair?"

Chris moved towards his desk and sat down. He smirked and thought, "Dang, she's good."

"Okay, so I'm thinking first that I need to have good communication with Michelle. If she feels supported, encouraged, and challenged by me, that's foundational."

Jennifer responded enthusiastically, "Yep!"

"Next, I'd say the running of the board meetings is

important. That means that I need to be disciplined to connect with Michelle a few weeks before each meeting. We can create a good agenda and get the information out in advance."

Jennifer jumped in and said, "I absolutely agree, but I'd add something." She hesitated and started up again with some obvious frustration in her voice. "Chris, board meetings were an area where I was disappointed in myself."

"Because of good old Robbie's Rules?"

"No, it wasn't that. But I still think having a basic understanding of *Robert's Rules* is a good idea. It was the fact that I had planned to do a better job of making our board meetings engaging and creative, pulling out the best of our board members and their knowledge to tackle issues and opportunities. I only did that…" she hesitated…"maybe 20% of the time. That's a disservice to our board members."

"So, what could you have done differently?"

"I could have made sure that during every meeting we broke up into small groups to tackle an issue. We could have done more to understand homelessness or create solutions to raise more funds. Things like that. Way too many of our meetings were just reporting on what has happened. The members could have read a report for that. Too many times, their greatest activity was saying 'aye' to some report. I'm embarrassed, and I regret that."

"Give yourself some grace, Jennifer. TCC made some great strides during your term as chair, and your legacy lives on."

"Thanks, but I hope you'll do better. Back to my question. So, what makes a great board chair?"

"Right. Good leadership with Michelle. And board meetings that capitalize on our board's talents. Third, I'd say that I must challenge and hold accountable our board members. That's not Michelle's job."

"Keep on," Jennifer encouraged.

"I, along with all the board, have to make sure we're being true—true to our mission, vision, values, strategic plan, and budget."

Jennifer didn't want to interrupt. She sensed he was on a roll.

"Then, if I could get the majority of our board members to be Ambassadors, we'd be kickin' it!" Chris exclaimed.

"Sounds like that would be a great year! Anything that you feel like you're uniquely gifted to do? Or that is instrumental during this season in the life of the organization?"

Chris thought a moment. "Yes, there is. Drawing on Sharp Edge and my background, I'd like to make TCC almost a household name in the Austin area. And I'd want to make it a city where homelessness wasn't a dirty word."

"That'd be awesome," Jennifer responded, now looking out over the cityscape of Buckhead with a smile on her face. "Anything else?"

"Well, Emily and I have been talking lately. I keep hearing her voice in my ear. Anything we can do as a board to encourage the TCC staff would be great. Their work is hard, so I'm going to meet with Michelle to see what would be meaningful and helpful. I'm going to try to do some things that might take a little of the TCC budget. I want to make a statement as a board that what the staff does is noticed and appreciated."

"Chris, I'm standing here with a big smile on my face."

He interrupted, "...and a coffee in your hand?"

"You know me well." She paused. "If you could accomplish

those things, I think it would result in a great year when your term is over."

"Thanks, and thanks for putting out the initial challenge. I'll never forget the day I got that email for our big meeting. I really thought I was losing my job!"

"Don't remind me of that little fiasco," she said, embarrassed.

"Seriously. I was such a skeptic!"

"Oh, I remember."

"While I am happy with how I've been able to make an impact at TCC, and more importantly in the lives of the homeless, there are a lot of benefits. I have grown in my leadership, just like you said. I've fostered some new friendships. Juan is a great friend now."

Chris looked at his new TCC pocket square.

"I honestly believe it's improved my marriage, too," he continued. "I think Emily likes me being engaged in this way. I sense I might be a little less selfish, too. I also like that Jayden is seeing me involved in the community, just as my parents were."

"It sounds like the initiative is going well for you, as well as the Sharp Edge team and our community...just like our leadership team had hoped for at that retreat years ago."

Chris looked at his watch. "I've got to run, Jennifer. Thanks so much! This was very helpful and so much more than I'd planned. Say, we do have a new capital campaign starting soon. I'll be sure you get a call about that," he said enthusiastically.

"And, I'd be thrilled to give!"

They both hung up.

Chris did a quick check of email and then dialed Michelle. She answered on the first ring.

"Hi, Chris!"

"Hey Michelle, it's Chris," realizing too late that she'd just said his name. He was nervous! "I'm looking forward to today's meeting. I was wondering if I could stop by about 45 minutes early and run over a few things with you. I just got off the phone with Jennifer, and it helped me to focus."

"Absolutely. I'll see you at 11:15," she replied. They said their goodbyes and hung up.

Chris walked into Michelle's office at TCC promptly at 11:12 a.m.

"Love that pocket square," she said, spotting the TCC logo and colors.

"It was a Christmas gift from Juan," he replied with a thumbs-up. "Thanks for the impromptu meeting. Jennifer asked me what makes a great board chair, and so I started thinking aloud and ended up making a list. I want to run it by you. See if you'd add anything, but also use it as my North Star for the year. Here it is, but not in any particular order." He worked through his list with her:

- Support, encourage, and challenge the executive director.

- Run great board meetings:

  - Prepare well in advance with Michelle.

  - Ensure information is sent well in advance.

  - Design board meetings that are engaging and creative:

    » Use small groups to discuss issues.

    » Help board members understand their role

and responsibilities.

- » Educate board on homelessness, board service, etc.

- » Create solutions for challenges like fundraising, events, etc.

- » Utilize their talents.

○ Challenge, thank, and hold board members accountable.

○ Foster the Ambassador mentality of board members.

○ Ensure that TCC is true to their mission, vision, values, strategic plan and budget.

○ Messaging:

- » Make TCC a household name.

- » Reduce negativity regarding homelessness.

• Encourage and show appreciation to staff.

"That's quite a list, Chris," Michelle surmised. "But I think it's very doable. Well, I'm not sure about the messaging part, but that's your area of expertise, not mine. I love it all!"

Chris took a deep breath and beamed.

She added, "If you do all of that, it'll force me to up my game, too. I want to do a better job of keeping you informed as the chair. But you've got a full-time job and a growing family, so I want to keep it at the right level."

"I'll tell you if it's too much."

"Deal."

Michelle told Chris she was pleased with how they were executing the strategic plan. Morale was good, and the services they offered to the homeless were considered some of the best in the country.

"I feel that I do a great job of leading the staff," Michelle confided, "but I need to give more energy to fund development and helping board members utilize their connections. There were too many times last year where I didn't follow up."

Chris thought about this for a moment.

"You remember when we first met in Jennifer's office?" Michelle asked. "That was the first time I'd met with a board member off-site. I still don't do that enough—going to their turf and getting into their world a little, meeting their people. All that to say, I love your list. And I'll be disciplined to create mine accordingly."

With that, they looked over the agenda one more time and headed to the board meeting. As they opened the conference room door, Michelle looked at Chris and said, "Let's go energize some Ambassadors for TCC!"

And they did!

◆ ◆ ◆

PERSONAL REFLECTION QUESTIONS FOR BOARD MEMBERS

Ask yourself the following questions and journal key points:

» What stood out to you from this chapter?

» How can you show support to your board chair?

» What are some ways that you can encourage or support the staff and executive director?

GROUP DISCUSSION QUESTIONS FOR BOARD MEMBERS

With a group of other board members, discuss the following questions and note key points:

» What could we do to make board meetings more productive?

» How might board members maximize the effectiveness of the board chair or executive director?

» What are some concrete ways that the board members can encourage the staff?

SUGGESTED ACTIONS FOR BOARD MEMBERS

» **Bronze:** Write a note of encouragement to each of the members of the senior leadership team of the organization.

» **Silver:** Volunteer for a difficult-to-fill position or leadership role, such as committee chair.

» **Gold:** Go beyond being a great board member and purpose to be an Ambassador for your organization every week.

Questions for Executive Directors and Board Chairs

CHAPTER 1: THE BIG ANNOUNCEMENT

» What are the benefits of someone volunteering with your nonprofit organization in addition to or in lieu of other types of volunteer work in the community?

» What untapped opportunities exist to partner with for-profit organizations that have a culture of giving and serving?

» How can you be sure that people don't have the same negative experience with your organization that Michael experienced with nonprofits?

CHAPTER 2: WHERE TO GO FROM HERE?

» What makes people excited to be on your board?

» What do you think is most frustrating about serving on your board?

» Do you make it a regular practice to connect with board members, other than at board meetings? Why or why not?

» What would be the benefits of meeting with board members at their workplace?

» What is, or should be, your board recruitment strategy?

» How could a board matrix help your organization?

» What could a board matrix indicate that you are lacking, considering your vision and goals for the coming year?

CHAPTER 3: LET THE ONBOARDING BEGIN

» How do you currently onboard (the process of integrating a new board member into an organization, helping them understand all facets of the programs, services, etc.) new board members?

» What do veteran board members seem to be lacking regarding making informed and educated decisions?

» What gaps did this chapter expose in what you are currently doing to inform board members?

» On a scale of 1-10 (10 being the best), how well do your board members know each other?

» Why would it be helpful if your board members knew each other better?

» How often do you invite those who receive your services to share with the board?

  • What benefits (current or potential) can you see from doing so?

» Do you regularly inform the board of statistics and data about the needs that you address?

  • How could equipping them in that way be helpful?

Chapter 4: Making Board Connections

» Why does board mentorship make sense for new board members?

» What goals should you share with mentors for your board mentorship program?

» What questions should new and existing board members ask each other at their initial meeting?

» How can you equip the mentors?

» How can you expand the connections beyond just the mentor and mentee to other key relationships (fellow board members, potential donors, key staff, etc.)?

Chapter 5: One Awkward Board Meeting

» What are some ways to make sure expectations are clearly set for preparation and participation in board meetings?

» LaShonda was praised in the board meeting for sharing and commenting on social media. What have you encouraged or praised recently?

» What are some behaviors that would be wise to praise? What could be the benefits of doing so?

» What role does *Robert's Rules* have in your board meetings? Are the *Rules* helping or hurting the flow and effectiveness of the meetings? How so?

» Have you reminded the board members of the procedures

you've adopted? How can you tactfully do that?

CHAPTER 6: FINDING THE FIT

» Are there any issues within the board that you need to address, but are procrastinating on doing?

» Have you clearly communicated expectations to the board related to both board meetings and serving/volunteering outside of board meetings?

» How can you leverage current events (news stories, movie releases, etc.) to engage more people with your organization?

» What would the benefits be of having one-on-one meetings with board members about specific ways they can serve the organization?

CHAPTER 7: RETREAT...AND MOVE FORWARD!

» What is the purpose of and potential benefits of conducting a board retreat?

» What would be the primary purpose of your next board retreat?

» What timing seems to work best when planning a retreat? Why?

» What should your role be in a retreat? What about staff members? What about board members?

» How, if at all, should you handle board members who do not seem engaged (showing up late, playing on their phones, etc.)?

CHAPTER 8: STEPPING UP!

» How involved should board members' businesses be with assisting your nonprofit?

» Are there any negatives to board members' companies being involved?

» What expertise do your board members' companies have that could add value to your nonprofit that you aren't currently tapping? (Be mindful of not just their industry, but their processes or stellar departments like HR, etc.)

CHAPTER 9: WHEN CONFLICTS ARISE

» Do you have a mechanism and/or policy in place to inform board members of tragedies or celebrations of fellow board members?

» Do you make it a point to reach out to board members during these difficult or victorious times? How?

» The show must go on! What can be done in the planning phases of a project to ensure it continues, even in the face of unexpected events?

» What do you currently have planned that could use more contingencies?

CHAPTER 10: THE AMBASSADOR

> » In your own words, what does it mean for a board member to be an Ambassador for your organization?

> » How can you increase the number of board members growing to be true Ambassadors for your nonprofit?

> » If a board member does not grow to be an Ambassador, what are your thoughts on asking him/her to serve another term (if allowed by your bylaws)?

> » If a board member goes above and beyond what is expected, how are they appreciated and recognized?

> » Do you have board members right now who have contributed significantly in some way and may not know how thankful you are for their contribution? If so, what do you plan to do about it and by when?

EPILOGUE

> » What stood out to you from the Epilogue?

> » What elements of Chris's to-do list as the new board chair do you agree and/or disagree with? What would you add?

> » How can you energize your board to be Ambassadors?

> » How are you preparing your next board chair for great leadership?

APPENDIX

Board Member Recruiting Checklist

Being clear up front when recruiting a new board member can increase the likelihood that the member will have a positive experience and that the organization will benefit from the member's service.

So, what should a potential new board member know before agreeing to join the board? Here is a list of basic information every recruit should know:

- [ ] Board service is a commitment.

- [ ] There will be an orientation process (and include the details of the time commitment and timeframe).

- [ ] Board members are expected to be present at all board meetings (add other events if those are required and add frequency and duration).

- [ ] Your voice will be as valuable at your first meeting as it is at your last.

- [ ] You do *not* need to know wealthy people to be successful. Each board member brings many unique attributes that make the board strong.

- [ ] Your passion for the organization must be greater than your fear of asking and serving.

- [ ] A monetary contribution by each board member is required, but you will determine how much you are able to contribute based on your personal financial situation.

Sample Board Matrix

TRAVIS COUNTY CARES BOARD

	Darius	Chris	Jennifer	LaShonda	Susan	Juan
Term Expires	2021	2024	2022	2024	2024	2024
Role	Governance Chair	Board Member	Board Chair	Board Member	Board Member	Board Member
Committee Assignments	Governance, Development	Beyond the Bridge, Marketing	Ex-officio on all committees	HR, Marketing	Development	Housing, Beyond the Bridge
Experience with Our Mission	X			X		
Board Leadership Experience	X		X		X	
Connections to Donors	X		X		X	
Nonprofit Board Experience	X		X	X	X	
Profession/Business/ Expertise	Wealth Management	Marketing/ PR	Executive/ Marketing	Attorney	Community Advocate	Construction/ Design

The Board Matrix should be utilized to ensure that you have both the diversity you need to represent those you serve and/or the broader community you are in. Different backgrounds and experiences bring unique views and insights.

The Board Matrix should not be used to create diversity just for the sake of diversity. It is important that all board members have a passion for your cause, a willingness to serve, an attitude of collaboration, and availability.

Email **info@coreinsightsleadership.com** for a blank Board Matrix.

Male	X			X	X	X
Female		X	X			
Race/Ethnicity	Hispanic	Caucasian	Black	Caucasian	Caucasian	Italian
Legal				X		
Finance/Accounting		X	X	X		X
HR/Recruitment/Training	X		X	X		
Development/Fundraising		X		X	X	
Marketing/Communications/PR	X				X	
Construction/Maintenance	X					
Strategic Planning		X	X	X		X
Age 25–34						
Age 35–44	X				X	
Age 45–54			X	X		X
Age 55–64		X				
Age 65+						

It is also important that you adapt this matrix to fit your organization. Make adjustments based on your mission, those you serve, your strategic plan, and the skills needed to make the impact you are seeking.

It is worth noting that demographic information is volunteered by the board members to the governance committee in order to gain diversity in perspectives and cultures.

Board Member Onboarding Checklist

You don't have to do all of these, but the more that you provide, the more likely your new board member will feel welcomed and prepared to serve at a higher level.

- ☐ Board mentor assigned to all new board members
- ☐ Board member's role and responsibilities
- ☐ Board expectations (attendance, giving, committee membership, donor recruitment, etc.)
- ☐ Key dates (board meetings, retreats, special events, etc.)
- ☐ History of the organization
- ☐ Most recent 990, budget and current financials
- ☐ Bylaws
- ☐ High level view of the strategic plan
- ☐ Staff and Board Organizational Chart (includes board committees)
- ☐ Contact information for fellow board members and key leaders
- ☐ Background information on the focus of the organization (e.g., homelessness, sex trafficking, educational attainment)
- ☐ Type of parliamentary procedures used by the board (e.g., how motions are made, use of consent agenda, etc.) and/or *Robert's Rules* cheat sheet
- ☐ Any legal or other significant issues that are current or pending
- ☐ Overview/review of minutes of a recent board meeting
- ☐ Reception for new board members and spouses
- ☐ See the organization in action

ARE YOU TRULY REACHING YOUR POTENTIAL? ARE ISSUES YOU'RE UNAWARE OF HOLDING YOU BACK? IS LIFE NOT TURNING OUT LIKE YOU PLANNED?

If you've ever been left out of an opportunity where you thought you could really add value, missed out on a promotion you believed you were perfect for, or seen a relationship deteriorate for no apparent reason, you likely have blind spots.

Imagine what you care about most in your life— your relationships, your work, and your community— all working more efficiently and effectively. What would it take for that vision to become a reality?

The answer has to do with how much you are paying attention to your blind spots. This book is about identifying and dealing with the behaviors, attitudes, and habits you're not even aware of that keep you from being and doing your best. We'll show you the hidden issues that are stalling your potential and teach you 11 proven strategies to overcome your blind spots.

Also written by **BRIAN BRANDT** and **ASHLEY KUTACH, PH.D.**

Core Insights works with nonprofits, businesses, schools, and ministries by providing a myriad of trainings related to communication, leadership, organizational culture, and personal growth.

If you're looking for experiential training on such topics as public speaking, 20 ways to build morale, conflict resolution, and much more let us know.

Additionally, Core Insights offers coaching, strategic planning, a speakers' bureau, and Dale Carnegie courses.

Call **903-534-1525** to discuss what we can do to help you make the greatest impact.

www.CoreInsightsLeadership.com

Acknowledgments

We could not begin to thank all of the people who have contributed to this book in one way or another.

However, we are both grateful to our spouses and children who bring us great joy.

Ann Terese, Jeremy, Katie, and Heidi Brandt are great blessings. Thanks for the love and support along the way!

Andy, Caden, Ryder, and Willow Kutach are troopers and have "rolled with the punches" through the past few years as I worked to complete my Ph.D., wrote two books, and changed roles within my career. Thanks for always loving and supporting me even though I'm sure you all think I am crazy for always taking on so many projects!

We're also grateful to our parents, siblings, mentors, colleagues, clients, and friends who have both shared ideas and encouraged us along the way.

Lastly, we want to thank all of the nonprofits we've volunteered or consulted with and the countless number of board members, board chairs, and executive directors we've worked alongside.

Made in the USA
Coppell, TX
16 January 2021

48298368R00107